# GLUE

## GREG "STORMIN'" GORMAN

"KEEPING 'IT' TOGETHER, TODAY"

"THE MOST REAL PERSON YOU'LL EVER MEET"

| Library of Congress Control Number: | | 2016919652 |
|---|---|---|
| ISBN: | Hardcover | 978-1-5245-6400-1 |
| | Softcover | 978-1-5245-6399-8 |
| | eBook | 978-1-5245-6403-2 |

Print information available on the last page.

Rev. date: 11/22/2016

To order additional copies of this book, contact:
Xlibris
1-888-795-4274
www.Xlibris.com
Orders@Xlibris.com
753642

# Contents

# Forward

This book is dedicated to all

the people—friends & family—who are

no longer with us here on earth, but always

in our hearts, watching us, protecting us

& reading this from above.

I actually started writing "Glue" in 2009,

& I had always intended on finishing it,

but--like many of us do--I procrastinated

...a...LONG...time.

In late December, 2015, I realized

I didn't want to have any regrets not publishing "Glue",

after everything I've been through in my life.

At 49, I decided to start living on my terms--& this is the start.

Being a parent, a coach, & a mentor is a great accomplishment…

However, after being the "glue" that keeps

EVERYONE & EVERYTHING in my life "together",

coming 'unglued' twice actually opened me up,

"saved me" from myself

& my thoughts I've always needed to share.

I've been through so much in life

that I thought my story could help others…

& as I finally share "it", I hope & pray it does.

"Enjoy the ride": here we go…

# PREFACE

# "Why?"...

I've always wanted to put my thoughts into words, you know, because I always have so much running around in my brain all of the time...

Oh wait…are you there? I know what you're thinking: who, what, when, where & why, right? WHO is this guy? WHAT is he thinking putting his thoughts into words? WHEN, exactly, did he find the time to come up with so many ideas, and scenarios in one brain? WHERE did this guy come from? WHY would anyone want to read a book by a relatively unknown like me?

The MAIN question we ALL ask in life is a 3-letter word, & there's so many answers to this one word…the word: **"Why"**. It could be an open-ended answer, long in form, or a closed-ended answer, where it might be one word, or just a few. But the word "Why" is probably meandering in our thoughts at least once an hour, each & every day. Why…3 simple letters, 1 word. We ask ourselves this word each & every day…Why me? Why this? Why that? Why now? Why then? It all starts with a 3-lettered question…WHY.

…& You're probably sitting there right now asking yourself, "WHY did you decide to write the book "Glue"? I used to be an English tutor while I was in college at Maryville, plus I wrote sports for "The Montage" at Meramec Community College. I decided to put ALL my thoughts into words & 'voila'…the next thing you know I have enough for a book that people can identify with. You want your writing to be invigorating, and not put people to sleep, or hit the "snooze bar".

Therefore, I hope that I not only "entertain" you, but you learn from me as well.

Some people may think of my thoughts as something you might read in a journal, or a diary. Well—to be quite honest--it started out that way & as I kept expounding further on everything, I showed it to my doctor & she said "you have something here…people would want to read this. It's up to you if you want to share it with everyone". Therefore, as I kept writing, I wanted to keep it on a "personal" level where people could identify with what I have to say.

The MAIN reason I wrote this book is for me, to do something for me, for once. All my life, I've given back to others, & now it's time to give back to myself, for my own well-being. I need to be honest w/myself & others, & start living on my terms before it's too late. I don't want to live w/any regrets in my life…at 49, it's time to start living, it's time for me to be "ME"…& that's "Why"? this book finally came to fruition.

As you sit there & soak in everything I have to say, I hope you don't necessarily look at this book as one of the typical 'self-help' books that you see in the bookstores. This book is more of an "autobiography" than anything, but one theme stands out: this adventure is one that is compassionate about life in general—growing up through the years, becoming a husband & father, and 'living & learning' through coaching

& life experiences—something that anyone & everyone can identify with: not your atypical "book" at all.

As you read my "rambling" thoughts on everything that's dear to me, I hope it makes you laugh & it brings a smile to your face. I also hope it makes you think & I don't expect everyone to understand everything I'm talking about, nor do I expect you to agree with everything I have to say. But as you read my take on things: whether it's what I've been through in my life, or my take on parenting & coaching in this day & age, or how I'd like to make the world a better place…I just hope you enjoy reading it & appreciate what I have to say. This is a dream come true for me & I'm glad you are part of it.

In the words of my all-time favorite band, Rush, I will always believe in the analogy of "Why" as well… "Why are we here?... Because we're here... Why does "it" happen?... Because it happens"... & as I always say on my e-mail messages to everyone: "Thank you for listening: God bless you all".

ENJOY "GLUE"!

# Coming UNGLUED...

# "Walk In My Shoes"

*"When faced w/a crisis, look upon it as an opportunity to grow as a person, to be stronger, & to face all challenges head on…"*

In life, we all go through our ups & downs...& each thing we experience takes "Glue" to keep "it" together, even when you feel your life is falling apart around you. "Glue" is needed for all of "the pieces of life's puzzle", in order for things to come together, "stick together", be one, & be whole. Once, as I was trying to reach out to a former friend via e-mail about my past life experiences, they forwarded a message to me from a Medical professional. AFTER this former friend shared w/ them what I had been through, THIS was their response(s) to me--& you'll see "why" I started to unravel & become "unglued"...

1st one: "Jesus! People like this shouldn't be allowed in society"

2nd one: What a WHACK JOB!!!!!!! This is very frightening. Is he sending these to multiple people? I bet the Dr. he saw for 2 hours enjoyed the hell out of that! OMG!!! I am floored!!!!

...THIS response by this person sent me "over-the-edge". My first thoughts were, "What a hypocrite! Medical people are supposed to understand & help others"...then again, I thought, "Maybe, I AM "dangerous", I AM "damaged". I felt I needed to "off myself" right there & then.

When I contemplated taking my life in 2008, it was as if I felt I had no more meaning in life. At age 40, I thought I hadn't lived up to others &/or my expectations & I was always feeling like I let down everyone around me. Receiving the message above didn't help either, therefore, I was set to do it. But--just at that moment, when I was ready to take a bottle of pills & go to sleep for good--I realized I had to keep living for my son & daughter: they are my world & always will be. I asked myself, "what would their life become IF I wasn't there for them?" THAT is what stopped me from taking my life: my love for my children.

I have what MANY today people have: Post Traumatic Stress Disorder (PTSD)...but I also have Eye Movement Desensitization & Reprocessing (EMDR) disorder, which is an information processing psychotherapy that was developed to resolve symptoms resulting from disturbing and unresolved life experiences. EMDR is rated in the highest category of effectiveness and research support in international guidelines for PTSD treatment. It uses a structured approach to address past, present, and future aspects of disturbing memories. Clinical trials have demonstrated EMDR's efficacy in the treatment of post-traumatic stress disorder (PTSD)...and as you read on throughout "Glue", you'll realize my PTSD is NOT military related...it ALL transpired from disturbing, and abusive life experiences.

In some studies, the combination of PTSD & EMDR have been shown to be equivalent to cognitive behavioral and exposure therapies, and more effective than some alternative treatments. Most clinicians use EMDR to solve various problems, and its research support is primarily for disorders stemming from distressing life experiences. During my past—especially while sleeping & dreaming—I've also had "**Premonitions**": a feeling that something unpleasant is going to happen; a situation when future events are foreknown or forecast. Combine all three of these symptoms, and what you have is something that's been stored away into my subconscious, since the doctors, and I discovered it in 2008. Through one medication, quarterly conversations with my therapist, and buying into the power of "positive thinking", I've been a more complete & inspirational person since 2009.

The **mental abuse** I've suffered during my childhood years & my adult years still haunts me to this very day--especially what some family members did to me...even physical abuse & (borderline) sexual abuse--I was part of & exposed to that as well. I've also been **bullied as an adult** as well by people I used to call "friend"—even 'loved ones'—that I thought I could trust too. It has taken a LONG time to "let it go"...& I'm glad I finally allowed myself to do so. The thing about **Bullying is it comes in many "forms":** it can be physical (punch, hit, kick), verbal/spoken (can be worse w/words, slander), mental (intimidation), cyber (computers & cell phones), written (malice) & through drug use (methamphetamine & heroin). What's more troubling is how if you defend yourself...IF you "retaliate" you will suffer more severe consequences that who started it. Defending oneself can backfire, whether it's kids, adults, etc. Also, "sticking up for others" can burn you as well when you don't have all the facts too.

During my first day at the Behavioral Health Center in 2008, I thought back over some crises in my life, & one common thread seemed to run through them. I emerged a little bit stronger, a little bit wiser, and a little more appreciative of the ways and methods of my Higher Power: GOD. I now realize that each proceeding incident presented me with two different choices: negative—"I should crawl under a rock and curl up and die"...OR positive—"I could accept this scenario as an opportunity for change with a new attitude toward an old, familiar situation". What really impressed me was that the choice was mine: It was up to me to decide which direction I wanted to take and which attitude I wanted to adopt. If there was doubt in my mind, I turned it over to my Higher Power: GOD.

During those days in Behavioral Health, I learned so much about myself as I was ALWAYS "Beating Myself Up Inside". On a daily basis, I found myself saying the following:

"I'm still hurting inside…"

"I let down my family…"

"I let down close friends…I've scared them!…"

But my doctor's said, "You're in the right place, right now!" I made friends very easily, but I was still emotional when talking about my past, especially the feelings & visions I'd had. **I'm still like "glue" for everyone else--ALWAYS "keeping 'it' together" for others--but I became "un-glued".** To this day, I STILL feel the need to apologize for what has happened with me through the years…& I always hope 'they' still respect me & can confide in me…

It's amazing how this one thing--one moment in your life--can define you, whether it's good, or bad. I've realized there's been many moments in my life, mostly good…but then there's that one time--that one night--just once, you make a bad decision, you don't think it out all the way, & **boom**--it stays w/you for the rest of your life. Even though some people have never walked in your shoes, or lived one second in your life, they'll judge you for that one instant, that one moment...for the rest of your life...& it doesn't matter if it's fact, or fiction...real, or fake...it's all about perception, & the way that person sees it in their eyes--& that's their conclusion, their "final answer", per se. I always exclaim to people when they meet me, "what you see, is what you get" & there are no "skeletons in my closet". I've left my door wide open for the world to see...it might not be pretty, but it's true, & it's real. Therefore, IF you don't like what's behind my door, then close it & lock it up...& leave me be.

I also learned that a guy like me can be in touch with my feelings & choose how I express them: *It is natural to laugh when happy, & to cry when sad*...even IF you're a Male. I can grow & change, & discipline myself to do what needs to be done. I also learned to not make mountains out of mole hills & look at problems as challenges. I sometimes envision myself as a character in a skit for "Monty Python's Flying Circus", where the illustrators would draw a picture of my mind opening up, kind of using a can opener to open up the top of my head to let out all of my feelings and emotions. I exercise every day—physically & mentally--& keep my 'antennas' (eyes & ears) up to identify what is positive every day. I must always remember I am growing and maturing each day in every way toward the good which is in me…**I am good!**

Some people still won't let me "let go" of THAT NIGHT--6/24/08: the last time I was ever "buzzed", "out of control", "on the edge"—& I almost died. I woke up in a hospital, not knowing what happened, but knowing that my life had to change—for the better. I thought I wasn't "good", that I was "damaged", that I "didn't deserve to live". That experience in 2008 at both Behavioral Health and Outpatient Therapy was unbelievably positive. You're very skeptical and hesitant when you enter an atmosphere as such. However, checking myself into a behavioral health center was the right choice at the time. It opened my eyes and mind to a whole new world I had never experienced before. It's very humbling, yet you become re-affirmed in yourself as a person, both mentally and physically. I learned from everyone--the patients, & the staff--that it's o.k. to admit to your faults and your negatives. The end result--you feel "cleansed", when you go through the process of becoming whole again.

After I arrived home from the Behavior Health Center & was beginning to start my classes with the Outpatient Therapy group, I decided to write to my closest friends…& this is what I sent:

"I'd like to thank all of you for praying for me & our family through this period. I've thought of all of you practically every day throughout this process I've been through. Speaking of that, the experience I had has been overwhelmingly positive. I can tell you now that I have PTSD (post-traumatic stress disorder), brought on by weaning myself off of my anti-depressant medicine--which brought on depression, & anxiety. Also, now I'm considered a "survivor" because of the abuse I was exposed to in my younger years. From the bottom of my heart, I really need to thank you all for your understanding of this situation I've been through & I hope you all can still respect me, confide in me, trust me & still consider me a lifelong friend. I love all of you—friend & family--and I look forward to moving ahead now."

...& this was just the beginning of learning how to stay connected, how to keep grounded...& how to stay "Glued" together, throughout my life.

# "D...is for DEPRESSION..."

*Drawing from Outpatient Therapy, Summer 2008, by me*

DEPRESSION...there are so many types of diagnosis, but everyone's experience w/it is different. For me, it's loss of appetite, not sleeping, "mentally" tired, restlessness & irritability, feeling withdrawn, losing interests in things I enjoy, plus your focus & memory are hindered (making decisions is damn near impossible when "D" hits). There's one thing you never want to reach: thoughts that life isn't worth living... IF you feel this way, THEN you MUST GET HELP. The most important thing one must remember is this: Depression Doesn't Discriminate--the "3D's"...it can happen to you, it can happen to me, it can happen to everyone eventually.

One thing I do when I'm feeling Depressed, is I write down a list of positives, a list of negatives... I weigh them equally & decide how to make the necessary improvements to make myself better. Consider my chart below... I use almost 24/7/365...

<u>Life "chart" for dealing w/Depression…</u>

<u>A "how to" Coping w/PTSD, Anxiety, Codependency…</u>
<u>& Triggers & Stressors</u>

**<u>(Triggers/Stressors)</u>**

- No space + No trust = "Suffocation"
- Heartbreak + Disappointment = "Disconnection"

**<u>(Coping)</u>**

1. Being w/pet (i.e. dog)
2. Writing

3. Listening to music

4. Watch TV (i.e. hockey, or "SportsCenter")

5. Talk w/someone I trust (i.e. children, spouse, parent therapist, best-friend)

When you suffer from depression, there are "triggers" that bring back memories that can make matters worse too. As some of you know, I was Catholic before I converted over to the Methodist faith in 1994. I received an e-mail, a "joke" actually, from a friend that showed a stain-glassed window with the image of two priests, and a young man, kneeling before the priest(s), with his head down—as if he was being "blessed". But his head was directly in front of the priest(s) groin area. The name of the joke was "Well, it had good intentions". At the time, I just shrugged it off, you know. However, I had a dream that a Priest I once knew was talking to me & a group of people, telling me about what he did to children, how sorry he was & how sorry he was that I was hurt so bad by things he did to others, & what my relative used to do to me. I know it sounds crazy, but that "joke" triggered the "memories" of what he did to others & what my relative did to me..& THIS is what it feels like to have PTSD, but mainly, Depression-- "triggers" are everywhere, & can happen at any time in your life...

Since I have PTSD & I'm a HUGE believer in "Paying It Forward" to others, I had a "Do The Right Thing" moment for someone once on Veteran's Day through a local TV station. I called to speak with a reporter who did a report on a former Navy Veteran who was denied service to two restaurants who were giving free meals to our former veterans. He needed his meal to be carry-out because he suffers from PTSD, Anxiety & fear of crowds. I told the reporter how I could identify w/this "stigma" towards those of us w/mental issues. Therefore, I put a $50 bill into the mail to the reporter to give to the man & his family to have a meal. It's the least I felt I could do to honor him & help heal both of us w/what we go through on a daily basis.

This leads me to another form of Depression I have: **ANXIETY.** Believe it, or not, EVERYONE has some form of anxiety in their lives--there's something that makes ALL of us uncomfortable, & it can also cause Panic Attacks in many of us...spiders, bugs, fear of heights, fear of crowds, etc. etc. MY top 2 are Snakes & Clowns: both freak me out, both take life-like forms too. Many people take on those personas & one day--if they don't watch out w/the way they are in life & towards others--they'll end up in a lake of fire. Therefore, IF this is part of your "personality", you might want to think twice about your integrity...& NEVER--I repeat... NEVER make fun of someone who suffers from

Anxiety &/or Panic Attacks... "learn to understand" & help out others who suffer from this...

Another thing I've battled w/for the longest time is something I call "S-cubed": **Space "Suffocation leads to Separation".** I've discussed this topic between our family & friends about "space & separation", & that we ALL need our own "space", in order to exist w/others. Some get it, therefore, they get me & what I've been through in life. I need "space" order to "survive"...to be a happy person, than the miserable, "suffocated" unhappy one they've seen in front of them for years. I need my next 25 to be the best years of my life, being me, being who I've always wanted & needed to be. I won't abandon anyone: I will always be there for everyone...but I will learn to take care of myself for once, as I've finally learned to love myself—it took a long time, but it's finally making sense. I thank God, for showing me the way, giving me the strength & courage, to be ME. I also thank those around me that have seen this in me & help bring it out of me. I just hope those of you reading this & those that have always been associated w/me will love me & accept me for who I am**...I'm finally "ME".**

Another thing I'd like to see more of on TV & social media is "creating awareness", & more talk of finding a cure for Cancer, for ALS, for Diabetes, &--ESPECIALLY--for more research & help for Mental Health "issues" that the majority of us struggle w/every day. I'm fed up that there's more time on TV recently for "male enhancement" products than there is for the concerns I mentioned above. It's bothersome to watch a sporting event these days & there's commercials for "boner pills" constantly & repetitively during the course of sporting events. Good grief! There's many families that sit down together & watch their home teams &/or national sporting events together &--in my opinion— there really needs to be a restriction on all of these advertisements.

There will ALWAYS be a **stigmatism in society towards mental illness & depression**: many people need to learn to accept it. The masses need to learn it affects the majority of the population—especially in the US--& it's invisible on the outside...that's why you never judge, especially if you haven't walked in others shoes. Furthermore, not all "demons" we face are bad, & not all angels are good, but not all histories are bad, & not all people are good. We have to fight almost every day, & we live through life as "safe souls." We breath, we live, we fight, & we bask through the bliss of reality. But in the end, it's okay...

As you read through this, you're probably asking yourself, "Why are you opening up & telling us all about your past--especially your battle w/Depression, PTSD & Anxiety--when you've never spoke of it before? Why NOW?" I guess it comes down to this: I was AFRAID to. I didn't know how people would react IF I came "clean" about my past, what I've done, what's happened to me, especially abuse wise.

Sometimes, it takes a person years to build up the courage to speak up, especially when there's so many subjects that are still "taboo" to some. Even w/all my flaws & imperfections, I've always admitted that I'm not perfect--I'm human. The one thing that separates me from others is the admission that I needed help... I was strong enough mentally to know I needed to reach out before it was too late. THIS, I defer to as **"Mind Over Matter"**.

Trust me when I say this... I KNOW people are going to judge me more now than ever before--it happens, it's part of the "territory" when you speak out with your voice, or--ESPECIALLY--on paper. **Depression is an "Invisible Illnesses"...**when people assume &/or judge, they might have no idea what you're battling. I've been called 'damaged', but now, I've been referred to as an 'attention whore' because I've spoken out about what I've endured. Furthermore, I came to a point of not "opening up" to anyone any longer, & completely eliminating anything that deals w/social media. People have really changed & it's sad: I guess I care too much about others. But THIS is what motivated me to finish what I started...EVERYTHING I've written NEEDED to be said, & I hope it will help you. As my Doctors said, "You have a story to be told to the masses: it will make a difference"...

# MUSIC: "Therapy for the Soul"

Music...it should inspire you...it should move you...it should be catchy & put a smile on your face. It's "therapy for the soul": the harmonies, the lyrics, the combination of instruments syncing together to become one—that's a beautiful thing. Music makes me think as well...the lyrics especially "speak to me" in ways only my brain truly understands. Combine all these elements into one, & it becomes one beautiful "whole"...the song.

Through music, I've learned through the years how to deal with many personal life experiences. For example, the song "Good Times, Bad Times" by Led Zeppelin, the very beginning verse really rings home for sure. When you break it down, it all makes sense, because "you know I've had my share" of the "good" & the "bad" times--ALL of us have in life for sure. For me, this style of song is therapeutic & speaks to my soul because it interprets my inward feelings in my heart & mind. Another one, "Heaven & Hell" by Black Sabbath, expounds on the good vs. evil perils we face in life every day. There's a softer side that gets to me too, especially "Fix You" by Coldplay, which resonates my feelings of what I've been through in life & in the present day. It's lyrically & sonically inspiring--it's "therapeutic"--and it helped heal me mentally after what I endured in 2008, and again in 2015.

Some bands & musicians are starting to mean more to me as I grow older & I watch my children grow up. Music needs to have "true meaning, true feelings" & not be hollow, goofy, or the silly crap that's out in the mainstream, or the overly serious stuff either. There are many other songs in my life that "define" me, & one that hits home for me now is "Doesn't Matter Anyway" by Greek Fire. There's a portion that makes me think of my "well being", & everyone else's for that "matter":

"Whatever happens, I'll be moving along

And I've gotta really learn to let go.

Everything is gonna be alright

Is something that I needed to know.

I'm letting it go,

The weight of this world.

Letting it go!

This gravity won't hold me no more!"

...it really hits home for me, & I hope you identify with it as well. Other songs have lyrics that hit home with me as well, such as "Broken,

Beaten, Scarred" by Metallica--it's 3 feelings I truly can say I live, & feel EVERY day of my life. There's so many others I can name, but "Breathing Lightning" by Anthrax, "Alive" by Pearl Jam, and "Xanadu" by Rush (recorded in one take: an 11+ minute song = pure musical brilliance), & two alternative bands--The Strumbellas & The Head & The Heart--are ALL songs & bands that I truly identify with always through their melodies & their provocative lyrics.

Then again, certain songs can tie a "philosophy" about the way you look at life too. One song I find very intriguing is by John "Ozzy" Osbourne called "I Don't Want To Stop"...& it has this line in it— "there's so many religions, but only one God". You know, there's a lot of truth to that lyric...there are so many religions available to all around the world & it's your choice how you want to worship. However, in all actuality, there really is only one God & one Jesus Christ...& as long as you go to church & pay your respects to God each week, I think you'll be OK. I feel that God has graced me in life with awesome friends & families...& I always "pay it forward" in praying to God each day & giving back to EVERYONE that touches my life. Then again, going to a place of worship might be your thing & that's how you find your own way to peace with God. All I'm trying to convey is DO NOT judge others when it comes to certain "taboo" issues, such as religion...

or sex, or politics--Everyone has their own way of finding their own "spirituality & identity" in life: mine is through music.

Through my love of music, I have always wanted to start my own band as well. I have a band "name" in my head & I think you will like it: LAST LINE OF DEFENSE...pretty cool, eh? You're thinking "where did I come up w/that?" It's an analogy, a saying, that's used in hockey for the Goalie...he's the "last line of defense" when the opposition is coming into the zone, past his Forwards & Defenseman, and he's the only one that can save his team from giving up a goal. This same analogy can be used in soccer, & lacrosse: any sport using a "goalie" as the last means of not giving up a point, or a goal. The main reason I like the name is because it reminds me of something "powerful", something that can handle "pressure" & make an impact on the "outcome/result"...

With as much as I love music, I have had the fire in my belly for years to write my own lyrics for recording artists. I've had a song on my mind for quite some time, but I've never quite finished it...the melody is there EVERY...SINGLE...DAY. It sounds like a Metal "ballad" that would be perfect for a reunion of Ozzy (Osbourne) & Zakk (Wylde). The song is called **"Dying Inside/Rise Up {guitar solo}/Coming Alive"**. The melody's there—I can hear the drums, the guitars, the voice of the Godfather of Metal...I just haven't finished the lyrics. The song focuses on depression, overcoming bad thoughts, & finding the light at the end up the tunnel…

This brings me to my final thought about music being "therapeutic"…& it involves my writing "tendencies". When I put my mind to something, I'm damned determined to do it, to finish things right there & then. One day back in June of this year, I was in the restroom, looked into the mirror & began to cry. I was thinking of what I've been through, what I've endured in my life…& I'm still here. I thought of a friend who helped me open up, tell my story, set my mind free…& within 10 minutes time, I wrote the following song: "Inside Me"…

(1st Verse) If you look inside/ inside of me/ you'll see a side/ the real me/ Reaching out/ it's so tough/ when you feel/ you've had enough/

You opened me up/ when I though I was done/ when everyone else/ had come & gone/…

(Chorus) You're in my head/ You're in my soul/ Always on my mind/ Truth be told/ You're in my heart/ beating bold/ burning red/ revived my soul… Inside me/ what you'll see/ a heart of gold/ the real me…

(2nd Verse) Three simple words/ I cannot say/ it pains me/ every single day/ I wanna say/ I cannot say/ God help me please/ I need to say

Without you/ there is no me/ Without you/ where would I be/ With you/ I've learned to pray/ To be grateful/ for every single day...(chorus)

(Interlude) I want to thank you/ from deep inside/ where all my feelings/ run to hide/ Maybe someday/ I'll open up/ & show you what's inside/ inside of me...(chorus) (repeat interlude)...

This song I wrote from the heart, as cried in front of a mirror, reaching deep inside my heart & soul. I couldn't believe how quickly & easily it came to me, as I thought about what I've experienced throughout my life--I finally had let go...& let God. It's amazing how someone can come into your life, make you be better & feel "whole" again--& I thank this friend for finally opening me up & letting out what's "Inside Me". My advice to ALL of you is this... IF you have something on your mind, something burning inside of you, & you want to express yourself, take pen to paper, think of a melody...& create your own musical interlude masterpiece from your heart--& share it with the world: sing it loud... sing it proud.

# The Top 100 Coach "GREGISM'S"

Through the years, I've come up with many analogies, thoughts & quotes that serve as motivators--not only in my coaching endeavors, but in life in general. Therefore, I not only decided to include these in "Glue", but I also created a separate work titled, "The Book of Coach Gregism's", available as a weekly engagement calendar. Some of my thoughts are light-hearted, some are serious in nature too...all I know is--for some reason--the players I've coached & my friends in my life have always enjoyed my take on anything & everything. Enjoy perusing through them my friends...

1. **Don't change for changes sake"**: make a change if it's to be better, or more positive. Some changes have a reverse effect, therefore, choose wisely.

2. "Life is great... Living it is better"...

3. "It doesn't matter what's right, or wrong, anymore—it's what one believes...**PERCEPTIONS** rule the mind now

4. **"The Fortnight Theory"**: Everyone wants "change for the better". Sometimes, things get better for a few days—then it

goes back to the same old, same old. IF you give it two weeks &--if nothing changes--it never will.

5. "Fairness" is one of the toughest words in life: it's the hardest to define due to the beholder's interpretation...

6. **Racism & hate** are "learned" emotions: they're not inborn, & sometimes these views depend upon your surroundings & how you're taught by your family & peers. Therefore, learn to accept one another for who each other are at ALL times...

7. Be consistent, not "Consistently Inconsistent"

8. "One you're satisfied, there's not much else to yearn for"

9. "Being talented is attractive, but being attractive is not a talent"

10. "Feeding the monster": when you're addicted to something, the more you "feed it", the worse inside you become...it just grows & GROWS

11. **Smiling & acknowledging one another is the best medicine for all**

12. **Beauty** is in the "eye of the beholder"...& it's more important "inside", than "outside"

13. **"Less is More"**: learn to live within your means...

14. Guide yourself over **"the hurdles of life"...** Sometimes, you jump high enough that you can clear anything that comes your way...then there's times you might stumble & fall. But it's a matter of picking yourself up, not giving up & doing it over again to make it all better. THIS is essential to life...every moment, every day...

15. "I have real strength & I'll be much stronger when all is said & done..."

16. People need to heed their own advice & "practice what they preach"...

17. In life, it's better to be a great listener than a great speaker: Listen to Understand, NOT to Reply...

18. "Cluttered house = cluttered mind...Clean house = clean mind"

19. "Everyone likes to give their "2 cents worth", but it's starting to become more like a Nickel, Dime or even a Quarter..."

20. "PITA" = pain in the ass

21. "Offense sells tickets...but DEFENSE wins championships"

22. **"Life's like a neutered dog":** don't get overly excited because someone &/or something will yank your chain & smack you right back into reality"

23. "Common sense isn't so common anymore"

24. One word that needs to be taken out of the dictionary: **"promise"**. Let's try not to use that word...say, "I'll do my best" instead. STOP with the promises—so many go unfulfilled and/or broken that they can really hurt and/or be devastating.

25. 'Honor God, Help People'

26. "From Adversity comes Courage, Confidence & Character"

27. Broken bones eventually mend, but a broken heart can last forever...

28. **"Leadership"**: for some, it's instinct...for others, it's a learned "process"...but the chosen always "make a difference" in the end...

29. **WISH**: Will + Intelligence + Skill + Heart--these 4 traits will lead you to the "Promised Land" in ALL of life's challenges...

30. "Coaching & Teaching" go hand-in-hand: I have strength, empathy & compassion for ALL of my players..."

31. Week 20 (May 14—May 20)..."**Once You Believe, Anything Can Happen**"...(Mantra for '13 MOIHA Jr. High State Champs)

32. **"IF there's such a thing as reincarnation, I pray I come back as a dog**. A dog loves you more than he loves himself--& that's my philosophy to life. No wonder **dog spelled backward is 'God'**—God definitely knew what he was doing when he created "man's best friend"…

33. "Healing" internally to be happy on the inside = **Ultimate Happiness…"**

34. "Keep the Faith, Hope for the Best, BElieve in YOUrself" are the essential keys in life for us all…

35. **In LIFE**, there are **Owls & Sparrows.** Sparrows: early to bed, early to rise does not always make one wealthy & wise. Most 'night owls' tend to have more brain activity & are smarter—it takes their mind longer to wind down at night as well.

36. **G.I.F.T** was our 2016 Team "Mantra"….

    **G**et "It" (BElieve In YOUrself)…

    **I**ntelligence (student of the game + play w/class + "intangibles")

    **F**…Focus (listen to understand): Finish (34:00): Family (respect for all)

Team (D-first, "gel", Work hard=Earn it)

...Life is a "GIFT"...& the 2016 season was definitely a gift from my players, their families, &--especially--from God, for giving me a chance to redeem myself & keep "living the dream"...

37. FULLY listen to understand, or you'll fall flat on your face... LITERALLY. IF you "burn bridges", you'll eventually find that no one will be there to help pick you up—or be "on your side"—when all is said & done.

38. **Depression doesn't discriminate: it can happy at any age, to any gender, to any creed, at any time in life...**

39. **"Some people in life 'get IT', some people just 'don't get IT', then there's some that just 'don't want to get IT'...& the latter group is growing larger day-by-day.**

40. A friend is someone who understands you, believes in you, and accepts you just the way you are.

41. "If you have much to say, & always hold it in, YOU CANNOT WIN. "Feed the need" to reach out, let it out, shout it out--if need be"

42. "I am one, I am whole, I am one w/my soul"

43. **"History can repeat itself"**. Therefore, tread lightly when it comes to your past "scars" because demons can arise again & you might be burned worse than before...

44. "ALWAYS keep believing, ASPIRE to dream & REACH for your goals, no matter what it takes to fulfill them"...

45. **Youthful exuberance** is a great intangible to have: it's a mindset, more mental than physical...if you feel you can do it, you can do anything...& age is just a number--you're only as old as you feel"...

46. The "mentality" of many people today: **"I want things to get better, but I don't want anything to change".** In order for something to improve, you can't have it both ways...

47. "Win with class, lose with class"

48. In life "do not judge" & think you "understand" EVERYTHING. Be careful of how you interpret ANY &/or ALL situations in life...unless you've walked in someone's shoes, you better make sure the shoe(s) fit, or you'll be literally stepping on toes, & breaking ankles.

49. Hearsay & gossip ruin so many things: most importantly-- friendships, relationships & TRUST...

50. If you take a group of 20 persons & make a statement, it will be interpreted 20 different ways. For example, put a group of people in a circle & whisper to the person next to you, "Jack & Jill went up the hill to get a pail of water"...& each person whisper's it to the person next to them. By the time it goes "full circle" & comes back to you, $5 says the person who originally started the chain will be told "Jack & Jill went up the hill & they made a baby"! I know—I'm being silly now! Well, not really...try it sometime with a group of people & see what happens—you'll be amazed at the final result!

51. "Never Say NEVER": you just NEVER know if &/or when something can &/or will happen in life...

52. Be the person people want to reach out to: be honest, sincere, & trustworthy...but be selective with WHO you reach out to—it must work BOTH WAYS...

53. "Learn to Love thyself..."

54. "No more fluff...only the good stuff!"

55. "First impressions, false perceptions"...it doesn't matter what's the truth anymore, it's what one believes...

56. Focus on the matter at hand: get into the "element", & be in the "zone"

57. "Age is just a number"

58. "People Who Always Think They Know Your Story Have Usually Never Finished A Book In Their Life..."

59. **"Things have become so politically correct that they're incorrect"...**

60. "CYA" = cover your ass

61. "There's a game we ALL play everyday...that game--it's called **"LIFE"**...

62. If people would "simplify", their lives would be easier. This analogy also goes hand-in-hand in sports & coaching: keep it simple for the players & don't complicate--that's a key for team success & to be on "the same page".

63. "Convenience" friendships = you're not a priority to others. It's better to be a priority to a few who love you, than an afterthought to many..."

64. Who are our "F.L.A.M.E.S" in life? Who are our Friends? Who do we Love & who Love's us? What Attracts us to one another? What is Marriage—is it 50/50, when it should be 100/100?

Who are our Enemies? (they do exist)...& who exactly are our Soulmates in life?

65. There's a saying that when you dream of someone, they were thinking of you before you went to sleep. I've always felt that seeing someone that day "triggered" your thoughts that night within your subconscious & that's why you dream about "them".

66. "At my age, you don't sleep around...but a nap always sounds good"

67. The only exercise some people get is jumping to conclusions, throwing others "under the bus", & pushing their luck...

68. **Don't ever sell yourself short: you cannot put a price on yourself...**

69. I've grown tired of three 'entities' over the years: Public utility companies, Health Insurance companies & TV providers-- they're the 'kings of loopholes & excuses'...

70. Sometimes, you might be better off saying nothing at all than speaking, because the spoken word can hurt deeper into the mind than your expressions &/or actions towards another. Be good, be smart, treat others ALWAYS as you want to be treated...with **respect**...

71. We are often caught up in our own little world that we forget to appreciate the journey, especially the goodness of the people we meet along the way. **Appreciating** one another is a wonderful feeling, therefore, don't overlook it.

72. One thing I firmly believe in is **"keeping it real"**: be true to yourself, believe in yourself, but be realistic.

73. **In the game of "life", you can never judge a book by it's cover, unless you've read the pages, & fully understand the story.**

74. Four words you should never say to your children: dumb, stupid, idiot, hate—they're the most mean & demeaning words you can say...

75. "Good will always prevail over evil in the end."

76. When you put power in the hands of the wrong people, a mess will ensue...let's just call it what it is: a "clusterf**k", with the potential for serious damages...

77. "Making changes for changes sake is the worst type of change..."

78. **"Mountains"** are one of God's greatest creations. When I think of them, I think of the peaks & valleys, which also pertains to life's daily adventures. There's been many of those moments in

my life, but I've learned through the years how to stay in the "plateau"--try to not get too up, or too down…& stay even keel.

79. Everyone is different & that's what's great about life: if we were all the same, we'd be clones…& that would be boring.

80. To me, the glass is always half-full—be an eternal optimist in life…

81. "Drinking & problems go hand in hand: when the buzz is gone, the problems are still there…"

82. I'm tired of being sick & tired… I'm especially tired of the disrespectfulness & ungratefulness of others--people are not like they used to be at all.

83. "The Shallow vs. The Deep": friendships take on one, or the other. The one's in the "shallow end" stay grounded, & don't take any chances for you, whereas the one's in the "deep end" will tread water with you, especially through the tough tides in life.

84. Everyone needs to **learn to forgive**, but you need to **never forget** as well. Move on & get past things, but keep "the experience" tucked into the back of your subconscious…

85. I want everyone to know that you're NOT ALONE & I'm here for you…FOREVER!

86. They say sometimes you can tell the **character** of a man by the way they treat animals, children & women. I wonder how I'm looked upon because I love all three of them & treat them with the utmost respect & accept them for who they are…

87. "Withdrawing yourself from others to heal isn't always the best medicine"…

88. "Be Selfless, Not Selfish"

89. Convey a positive attitude at all times with family, friends & everyone you encounter in life: be caring, sharing, thoughtful, thankful & respectful--learn to love, & appreciate EVERYONE & EVERYTHING…

90. "It's all good"

91. Be nice to one another, appreciate one another—this "ethic" is **THE "Code Of Life"**…

92. "You cannot help anyone, unless you help yourself first"…

93. "THIS is my life: it's not perfect…but I wouldn't want it to be any other way"

94. **"Imperfections make us all uniquely original..."**

95. "Don't ever "lower yourself" to other's low levels of standards & behaviors..."

96. 'Don't get "too up", Don't get "too down": find the "Gray" between the "Black & White"

97. **"I care, therefore I share"**

98. "I firmly believe that God sends "signs" by having certain people cross our paths in life for a reason: to help save & heal one another's hearts & souls...

99. ALWAYS have one another's back, ALWAYS be there for others on their toughest days, to pick them up, inspire & motivate them, & ALWAYS hope & pray for the best for EVERYONE

100. The world we live in today is not easy: Meet your challenges head on & always do your best. Just saying "I can", instead of "I can't", can motivate something deep down we all have: **HEART**...it sometimes rules our minds, but it's the one thing that gives us the inspiration we all need to be all we can be...


...NOW, wasn't that fun, or what!

# What is "Life"?...—10 SHORT STORIES

## *The world "through my eyes"...*

*McKenna (2), Colin (6) circa 2005*

It's amazing sometimes the thoughts that run through my mind. Sometimes, I chuckle, thinking about something my son &/or daughter said/did during the day. That "thing" alone is what I love about life—"looking through the eyes of a child": most of the time, their thoughts & beliefs are innocent, but they can be brutally honest. For that, I thank God that they are the future, that God grants life always w/ good intentions. Children remind us that we're all born into this world equally...after that, you're on your own & it's what you make of "it"--LIFE. Some are born into royalty, some into poverty...but the **"richness of life"** is what's inside your heart & mind--be happy, be grateful, be respectful...that is the key to being "whole".

Everyday, I also think about the things I see, or encounter during the day & then I shake my head—what is this world coming to? Why can't we all just get along & respect one another. Through my eyes, I prefer to leave most past experiences there... "in the past". I'd rather not re-visit "why" something didn't turn out well, therefore, it's my view when it comes to relationships too. There's a reason "why" things didn't work out the first time around, so "why" put yourself through those same feelings & emotions again...I prefer not to be burned twice for the same reasons & actions from before. I like my experiences to be "cool & calm", not "hot & bothered".

I'm not one to say "I want to change the world" but I do want peace in this world & things to be better going forward in life. The saying, "All the world's indeed a stage", every second, every minute, every single day is SO true. They also say you "die another day" too, as each day is one less day you have here on planet earth. In my mind, every day is a new day, & it's what you make of it...so do your best—ALWAYS.

**"Fitting in" today** with others is something else I ponder. For example, if you meet up with family, &/or friends & you haven't seen some of the people in a long time, do you find yourself feeling "out of place", or "disconnected"? Honestly, I think we ALL feel this at some point & time. It's also amazing to see how others have changed--whether it's for good, or better...but some never change--& they never will. I ask myself daily, "where do I "fit?", or "where do I "belong?" now. But, God willing, I'm finding my way—that's for sure. So many things have happened in my life, some things that I thought would never rear their "ugly head" surfaced again too. But I've figured "it" out on my terms—I was finally be able to finish "Glue" with my head held high to present to the world.

Sometimes, I also feel like an **accessory** in life! When you go shopping at the mall, you tend to accessorize—adding things along the way, piece by piece. When I say "I" feel like an accessory, it means I'm "along for the ride", or "fill in the blank" with me. When you're with your family and/or you're with a group of family members, I am "the husband", "the father"—kind of like being seen, not heard. I'm "only along for the ride", I'm only there because I have to be there—to fill

38

in the blank. Whether you're a man, a woman, boyfriend, girlfriend, husband, wife, and especially children—boy and/or girl—we all fit in that "fill in the blank". One thing that is certain—I'm never an accessory with my children: they love their Dad unconditionally.

But there's another thing that we ALL should remember as we look around us each day: **as much as there is negative in this world, the actual positives outweigh them**. I always strive to be positive at all times, but it's not easy. If something is wrong, or something needs to be corrected & made right, I do it tactfully. There's no need to raise your voice, jump up & down &/or scream: do it peacefully & everyone will work together better...& one other thing: **PLEASE do not exclaim to others, "I know how you feel"... NO, you don't**. We all look at things differently, we all react & respond differently--no two people are alike. Just remember that when you speak w/others, be "cognoscente" of what you say, & respect their emotions.

**IF people were more like dogs, the world would be a better place.** Dogs love unconditionally, are grateful, respectful & protective of their mates...hence, why do you think Dog spelled backwards is GOD? There's a reason for that: trust me...

...Once, as I sat on a Sunday afternoon--the Lord's day—a thought crossed my mind: in my heart, I'm sad, & I'm miserable. How is it that I put on this "facade" to others, always being positive, always encouraging

& uplifting to others, yet the pain inside me is sometimes so engrossing, I don't know how I "mentally" make it from day-to-day without losing my mind? Some things get old, yet we put up w/it... EVERY... FRIGGIN'... DAY. WHY do I do it? My answer: **I'm just like a dog—they love others more than they love themselves**. I love people, I love life—in general—but the lack of respect, the ungratefulness, the "begging" for help from loved ones & it goes unanswered—& it gets old.

As I finished "Glue", THIS—putting my "feelings on paper—is my ONLY way to "reach out" & show you what my eyes have seen...& NOW, everyone will know even more about me than ever before, but I'm perfectly fine with that notion, & those feelings.

## "Oh NO: It's one of those "taboo" subjects—UGH!" Politics

One story I love to share is one that takes my back when I was first a parent & we still lived in South County in St. Louis. I was at a polling place & some people of the "older generation" were talking in line. I'm not an eavesdropper, but I couldn't help hearing this "statement" by a an older fellow American: "you know, I want things to get better, but I don't want anything to change"...huh? Still to this day, that one statement still stumps me: really? How can something—anything!—for that matter "get better" w/o some sort of "change" taking place.

While we're at it, let's just throw out the political "labels": Democrat, Republican, Liberal, Conservative. To me, politics is almost like an individual sport: they represent themselves, not an entire party and/ or team... they're all individuals with their own thoughts, ideas & agendas. Call it "Team Bill" or "Team Bob" because not every person is going to have the same viewpoint(s) just because the say they're "Left Wing" or "Right Wing". I personally feel it's all bullshit to begin with. The one thing—no, the one word—that politicians use that they should throw out of the modern-day Dictionary completely is "Promise". I cannot stand that word & I never try to use it. There are so many broken, empty, unfulfilled promises made by politicians--& people in general—that it shouldn't be used, whether written and/or spoken.

## Religion

No one is perfect—that I know. But one thing I don't like to hear is how hypocritical some 'Self-Righteous' people can be. I believe in God & pray every day, I try to go to church when I'm able, & as well as my other family members. But I've grown tired--& others have too—of these ones that think if you don't regularly attend church and/ or contribute monetarily to the church, you're not being "faithful". Faithful? How about the actual faith-'less', who think they can 'buy' their way into heaven, & that they're better than you because they have more access to monetary contribute. There's too much of that—everyone should be realistic in their gifts & tithes, & the way they choose to "worship" their Lord & savior, Jesus Christ. The worst part of all: when one of these people has the mentality of 'do as I say, not as I do'…especially when outside the confines of the church walls. I can give you many examples of people who break the 10 Commandments every day—especially adultery & stealing. I'm not trying to point fingers—I just don't want people implying they're 'holier than thou' when they're mortal & human, just like you & me.

## "Selling Out"…

One thing I've learned through the years is to monitor my health better, especially "internally", in order to keep myself "glued" together, & functioning properly. I was diagnosed w/a **Fructose Intolerance** in 2011: It's in so many foods that you don't realize it until AFTER you've digested something & it doesn't agree w/you. But what makes the situation worse is the "artificial" version, High Fructose Corn Syrup, is ruining the insides of most of the people on the planet. So many companies are using it in their products that it's making us all—literally—sick to our stomachs. My personal feeling is that they're by-passing using real Sugar because of the bottom line for their corporations and/or the stockholders: more profit w/substitutes.

This is an epidemic around the world—I'm sorry to be harsh, but this is why so many people have allergies to foods (including my daughter, who has a Peanut allergy). The chemicals we're digesting, ingesting & breathing in as well (allergens), are hurting us all. When we were younger, we didn't have all of these allergies & allergens. I feel the FDA needs to be firm w/the producers of all food products because it's creating a 'downward spiral' effect in our 'internal systems'. One thing that stems from these intolerances: it's not only a physical deficiency, but it becomes mental too, because of the stress it puts on your body & mind...you become a "prisoner" of your own body because you don't know what's safe to it, & how your body is going to react to it.

The **"Gods of Greed"** ...it's a thought (& a song I'm writing) that's ALWAYS "running through my brain", because I don't like and/ or respect companies, or organizations, that have their own hidden "agendas" & what they want us to believe is their "gospel" of mistruths. I'm so tired of things being politically correct that they're incorrect, that companies "sell out" to make profits for their shareholders at the expense of us ALL, & that there are "Loopholes" lurking around every corner, in every contract that's spewed out these days. There's not much that gets me mad, or my blood boiling, for the most part, but there's one that I cannot stand: the arrogance of upper-management & the evil destruction that the almighty dollar has ingrained into the souls of manufacturers across the globe…THIS form of thinking needs to end before we're all broken, we're all in despair, & we all lose hope.

## Social Media & "Modernization"

One thing that absolutely floors me—everyone says you need to get **"modernized"**: use cell phones, e-mail, texting, social networking. Then, when you get a new device & try to contact someone, they don't respond back! That I don't get at all—why have it? I actually prefer talking face-to-face w/people—anyone & everyone—for that matter. I don't like to talk on phones either—whether it's a cell phone, or the "old fashioned" cordless phone, or "prehistoric" land line, God forbid. I hope you all understand what I'm trying to convey here. There's a **lack of "real" communication** between all of us & we need to rewind back to what we all first learned to do as an infant: how to speak to each other.

In regards to social media, I believe in "technology etiquette"— **"R&R" = Read & Reply, or "A&A": 'acknowledge' & 'appreciate':** don't put off your family & friends…if they took the time to contact you & write to you, it's only proper to reciprocate. When it comes to social "networking", if someone sends you a friend request, feel honored that they want to share their life with you, as much as they want you to open up to them as well. I learned that right away when I joined. Don't hit the "ignore" prompt: that's just inconsiderate & mean. Plus, if they write on your "wall", acknowledge it please! Use your manners & write back to them as well: the same goes for any messages, like e-mail: respond back—NO excuses! We're all busy but you shouldn't be too busy ever for a friend & especially your family.

Throughout time, my life has become an "open book" too: there's no "skeletons in my closet". I like everyone for who they are...& sometimes, the feelings are not mutual from others--I've seen it & felt it personally from others, especially through **social media**. Does it hurt? Sure: I have feelings, I'm not perfect--no one is...but some feel they are. Many people go on social media sites & act "10 Feet Tall & Bulletproof"... I feel some of them would s*** themselves IF they actually had to face someone in public that they throw under the bus repeatedly. IF you have a problem w/someone, do it in person--not on a keyboard, or "word of mouth".

What I'm really trying to stress is that there's more "vices" than "virtues" today. Honestly--it's overwhelming us all & hindering society as a whole. There's too much "stuff "...is "more" really better? NO! There's too many "distractions" today & so many things are "out of focus" now than ever before. Therefore, I feel "old school" is better sometimes than the "new school" way of life today.

**In Summary...** I do not like, nor respect, people who insist on telling me how I should live my life, &/or raise my children. My answer to them is this... "Once you make my house payment, or car payment, or buy my family their wants & needs, then you can tell me what to do... until then, mind your own business, limit your comments, or--better yet--shut the f*** up!" Everyone's entitled to their own opinions & beliefs, & I respect that. But PLEASE don't push them off onto me--I don't do it to you, therefore, respect works both ways: show some class & dignity in your life & abide by what I said. Especially, IF it pertains to politics, religion, sex &--especially w/me--music &/or sports.

## "Attention, shoppers: PLEASE check in your EGO at the door..."

In today's world, people are not what they used to be...especially, out in the public eye for ALL to see. It's amazing some of them stay "glued" together, when—in reality—they're "unglued" from the inside out. People have a nasty habit of being 'ungrateful, selfish & self-centered'. Some people I know only know you when they need &/or want something. I have an idea for these types of people—they should change their answering machine and/or voice mail to the following:

"Hello. I will not take your call right now because I'm too pre-occupied to speak to you. I will talk with you only when I need something from you for me because that's the way I roll, you know. It's all about me, myself & I & if I need/want to talk w/you, you have to wait to hear from me. Thank you."...

So many have become this way that I personally feel you're better off speaking face-to-face to get anywhere in this day & age. Just saying…

One thing that really amazes me in this day & age is how **"superficial"** people have become. People have become much more shallow & not as deep as they used to be: that's really sad—it's a shame actually. You see it is particular these days in many businesses. For example, the restaurant business has trended this way—whether it's fast food, or a sit-down restaurant…this type of "persona" has taken shape. When they say "Hi! How Are You?", just tell them "I'm fine" & move on—they don't want your life story: they just want your order, collect your money, serve you your food & say "Have A Nice Day!"—better yet "Have A Nice Life!"—and move on. Just when you think you get to know them, you realize you're just a customer, they're an employee providing you a service. The only ones who care are the owners & General Managers—they're the ones that matter & really care about you. It's a shame but it's how they make you feel. I've always tipped so well to people because it's a hard, thankless job sometimes: "serving the public".

It would also be nice for others to **reciprocate back** & feel like you & your family are of value to him/her. If you & your family aren't buying "the products", then they don't make their living. Think about it…I'm not trying to slam anyone but there needs to be more of a "mutual respect" between the customer & the employee. We've had our share of great waiters & waitresses that have become like family to us because they take the time to do it right. You should always reward them with great gratuity because they've provided you one of your biggest needs in life—a hot meal for you & your family. There's an aura regarding customer service skills that exists in this this day & age in so many corporations & businesses because of the atmosphere, the expectations, the surroundings: you name it! It's everywhere, especially in telemarketing: another thankless job that's unbelievably hard to sell & convey to the public. So many businesses treat their employees like freaking robots—it sickens me! They make you feel dispensable—you'd be better off being your own boss or traveling abroad than to put up being treated inhumanely.

Don't you love how "**customer service**" is conducted in this day & age. It's hard to find people for these jobs & much of it is done in 'broken' English. I also love how the operators at businesses and/or corporations have such a "laissez-faire" attitude on the phone. They sound like they're only there to collect a paycheck & they really don't care about taking care of your needs. Don't get me wrong—some people really care, but there's a minority of workers that don't care & don't really "want" to get "it" at all. Therefore, let's create the "SMELL

Factor": Stop Making Everything Look Laissez-faire…everyone needs to start caring & take a stand to make a difference.

People need to stop w/the **"attitudes & egos"**…or, as I term it, the **"A&E Principle"**. We're all tired of ungratefulness, selfishness, ignorance, arrogance & cockiness…& especially "trash-talk" & "talking smack". I feel that everyone should look at themselves in the mirror & accept themselves for who they are: love yourself for who you are, but don't push yourself on others: humbleness is the key to life to be appreciated. Another aspect of life that's become tiring is **'entitlement'** by others: they say what they want, whenever they want—they're not responsible for their actions & feel they should have no repercussions, or "earn" anything—just "gimme, gimme, gimme". Only small minded people feel this way when it comes to things in life, but IF you work for EVERYTHING, then you'll deserve your rewards & appreciate life & what it entails more.

Oh, what I would do to make things better for everyone…I just want everyone to get along ALL THE TIME. I know I'm asking for a lot here, but PLEASE reach out when you can: you never know when you're going to make someone's day better. It will make you feel better as well by "paying it forward" by dropping your pre-conceived notions of how people should be & accept one another as you would want them do the the same for you--let go, let things be & treat each other fair & as "equals".

## Those three "magic" words...

I have a hard time saying, **"I Love You"**, because of all of the traumatic events I've experienced in life, the abuse I've taken--especially emotionally—& I don't want to let anyone else down, as I've been let down numerous times. I do unconditionally love & accept EVERYONE, in particular, my family, friends, & my "Hockey Family". Why does it take so long for ALL of us to **"open up"**, & let our real selves & feelings show? Because...we're tired of being let down, being misunderstood, that we **"hold back"** & down want to let anyone else down &/or bring them down w/us. We attempt to remain upbeat, but--deep down--we're so broken inside & disappointed that we cannot "let go & reach out" to others. THIS "consumes" us...each & every one of us...

I've also realized in my life that you cannot control another persons emotions &/or how they react in certain situations. It doesn't matter if they're young, or old, male, or female, everyone reacts differently, & all you can do is simply accept that's how it is. I will always treat people w/ respect, kindness & dignity, because that's how I was raised, & that's how I roll...just don't expect it to be a "two-way street" because others my not be "programmed internally" the same way you are. I will also say it/s nice when you "pay it forward" & you're appreciated: it's a great feeling when someone "gets it" because they get you.

I think we also wonder to ourselves at times, "what have I done to deserve this?" in life, whether it's good, or bad. When I think of the "good", I think, "why do I have such a great, solid group of friends, who are there for me, especially when I didn't know if I'd ever find the light at the end of that tunnel". Then again, I also wonder about the ones who say I'm "broken" "damaged" & "challenged". All I know is that the "former" group is my "rock", the "latter" group is small, yet destructive--but the former inspires me every minute, every day. I thank ALL of you that truly say "I Love You" to me, but—for me—it's hard to say "those 3 magical words", but I do "love"--the feeling's mutual...I just can't say "it".

# Aww...that's so sweet :) ...

*My buddy, "Ty Ty"*

To further continue the preceding short story, one thing that has become a two-way street for people to convey their "true thoughts"... is **Compliments**. Since I'm a coach, mentor & father, I prefer to give them, however, it's tough for me to accept them. I always like to inspire others, make them feel good & make them believe in themselves. However, for me, I'm humble & I appreciate them...it's just tough for me to accept them because I don't always feel I'm "that good". Because of my life experiences, I can't help wonder IF I'm doing the right thing, or not, sometimes.

I will also say this: compliments are a way of sharing a "positive" w/ someone, but--for some unknown reason--in today's world, some people are offended by them. Whatever happened to the "motto", "if you have nothing good to say, then say nothing at all". I'd rather be positive than negative, but this is the world we now know... God forbid for being nice, & treating people the way you want to be treated.

One thing I won't pass up doing between now & the end of my life is telling those that matter to me most how I feel about them. I'll find the courage to say what I want to say, & be honest w/myself & to others...& if/when someone compliments you, or reaches out to you, savor it. Sometimes, it truly is God's way of sending a message that certain people in life were meant to cross paths: I've lived it, I've experienced it & I'll be forever grateful for them for doing it. Be kind, & be genuine in return, because they were there for you...& always "pay it forward": not only for them, but for everyone you encounter on a daily basis.

# Be You + Be Real = Be TRUE...

*McKenna in her "element"*

Sometimes, things in life have to make a "full-circle" in order to turn an unfortunate situation into a great ending. At times, when I'm all alone, I enjoy it, I soak it in...I appreciate the quiet, in order to sort things out, put things into perspective & to "think straight". However, there are those times where I'm putting on a facade to make everything on the outside look great, while--deep down--I hurt so much that I'm dying inside. It's a feeling I can no longer hide, but God knows I try. More than anything, the heartache hurts more than the mind, or the gut can take.

It's best to **tell the truth**, even though you might hurt yourself & others around you. You shouldn't be ashamed of yourself either. If you've done something wrong, come out & express it & admit it, because--in the end--people will admire you more if you do. There's nothing wrong in admitting you need help either: people will look at you as a stronger person if you do...& God knows we've all done things in life we regret. But if we atone for our mistakes, admit our faults & try our best to be better, we can learn to live w/ourselves, & hopefully, others will accept us for what we really are: HUMAN. I've done many things in life that I look back upon & say, "what was I thinking? Why did I do that?" I think EVERYTHING we do is a "lesson learned" in life, each & every day. That's why I feel you can learn something new every day--whether it's good or bad, negative or positive. Just be...

**Making a necessary change** can be "cyclical" too, as some things have to "cycle themselves", as in going through adversity before being rewarded. They also say, "good things come to those who wait": **IF you**

**Keep the Faith, Hope for the Best, &--always--Believe in Yourself, everything shall fall into place & work itself out**. The main thing I'm conveying is to be true…to yourself & to others. To be a real friend, you must be kind, yet fair, but wise. I've seen many, many people hurt lately--words can really hurt sometimes, & you NEED to hold yourself accountable for your actions. If you don't, NO ONE will respect you. Wouldn't you rather treat people the way you want to be treated? I always strive to be positive, nice & respectful to everyone: man, or woman, young, or old. PLEASE: let's appreciate one another--always.

## What ever happened to R-E-S-P-E-C-T?

You know what's starting to drive me insane: the **lack of respect** by people, especially life in general. Sportsmanship by people is getting worse & worse by the minute, especially as I watch the World Cup right now & I see people doing flips after scoring goals when they're up 4-0.

Honestly, as much as I feel I try to help out people & respect them unconditionally, I feel like I let down people as well. Do you ever get the feeling that no matter what you do, you're never going to make everyone happy, or ever be satisfied? It's amazing how sometimes you're the one that's always wrong, & needs to change. I feel that way sometimes, just like Charlie Brown always does.

Another thing that saddens me more than anything else is this: I'm very real, I'm very deep—I show emotion because I care. I care more & more each day about what happens in my life & the people that surround me, whether they're family or friends. I just wish sometimes people would have a **"mutual" respect** for one another. It even happens to me sometimes every day where I feel like I'm always giving, giving, giving, which is just my nature—all I ask for in return is a simple "thank you", or "I appreciate it and/or you & what you do". I don't ask for much.

One reason why I've always felt that I have a good perspective on **"reading" people** is that, at the age of 19, I became an intern for Anheuser-Busch. Trust me when I say it can be very intimidating being in a corporate "atmosphere" like that at such a young age. However, as you get to know people, you realize that we are all the same in one aspect: we all have a need to be accepted by others. That's why, no matter what you're age is, you should feel comfortable enough to be in any "circle" of people. I feel the same way about race(s) & genders as well: everyone should try their best to get along, be positive, but most of all, accept one another for who they are & not be judgemental—as the saying goes, "never judge a book by it's cover".

**People must be held accountable for their actions—& bring back "mannerisms".** IF people, young & old, male & female, would just think--better yet--use common sense before they say &/or do something they might regret, this world would be a lot better place we live in. Until the day comes when this happens, we--as a society--will always have this "flaw". **Being judgmental is one of the worst "habits" many people have too.** It leads to offending people & can cause serious depression issues for the person offended & the person saying it. It can become a "downward spiral" personality flaw that leads to self-esteem issues for both parties involved. If people would learn to put forth kind "gestures", say "thank you", & learn not to "judge" a person on their appearance alone, life would be so much better. The little things in life mean so much to me...paying another person a compliment like 'have a nice day'...being around friends & family...giving people hugs—that's what humanity should be about.

Therefore, THE main thing I suggest to do is **reciprocate back to people** because of my deep respect for other people. Even IF you can "feel" that the other person just doesn't feel the same way about you that you feel about them, that's ok—be the better person. I know it's a sad feeling because I like everyone & I'm always going to treat people the same way: whether they're male, or female, a young person, middle-aged, or an older adult. If there's one thing--one "mantra"--I can offer to all of you reading this book, it's this: **treat one another with dignity & respect & you will see "results".**

# Niceness + Happiness = Inner Peace...

*Illustration by my daughter, McKenna*

"<u>**Sad**</u>"...it's one of the worst feelings we ALL experience. This emotion can come on at any time & it really "dampens" your spirit. It can drag you down into a "dark hole" IF you're not careful, especially

IF you dwell on what brought you down. For me, one thing to lift my spirits is the love of my dog: pets love so unconditionally & heal us in their own way(s), whether it's the wag of a dog's tail as they stare into your eyes, or a cat curls up into your lap & affectionately purrs. Sometimes, we all need this kind of "therapeutic relief" to keep our sanity, & God knows I need it daily...what about you?

...so, then, bears the question: What is **"Happiness"?** Well, for me, IF you can wake-up each morning, look into the mirror, & your happy w/yourself, & the life you're leading, well, GOOD FOR YOU! I feel there's so many miserable people in this day & age, plus so many people leading "double-lives" that--IF I were a betting man--I would probably be rich IF I bet on how bad people feel inside, or how they put on false representation of themselves...every...waking...moment. What we ALL need to get back to is this: being HAPPY.

John Lennon was once posed a question in a class when he was a young man by his teacher... "What do you want to be when you grow up?" Most young boys his age would say, an astronaut, a policeman, or some successful person... John's answer: "Happy". The teacher told John, "You didn't understand the question, John!... John's response: "You don't understand life."...

To this day, that quote has stuck w/me my entire life. It's not easy to be happy all the time, every day...but, as I say, you can always find something good in every day--find the gray between the black & the white.

Through the years, I've learned that there's a difference in being **"nice"** & "too nice" in life. Niceness can be defined as "respectful", or "caring". Then again, being "too nice" can really bite you in the booty: God knows I know. I believe in treating others the way I'd like to be treated. However, those same feelings are not reciprocated quite often... others are not like you, or me. The worst feeling is when you go out of your way for someone & they're so ungrateful, & they can expect more sometimes too. When you finally get the courage to say "no", they look at you like you have two heads & discard you like a broken-down car in a pile of scrap heap. Yes, I feel this way often & it's probably why I feel so awful about myself & get hurt by others actions sometimes. Maybe, IF I was more of a "prick", my life would be better, but my subconscious would be beating me up inside my head. Either way, it's hard to "win" at the game of "emotions" in life, & I ALWAYS wear mine on my sleeve.

People are not what they used to be. You might be kind, sincere, genuine, complimentary. BUT, do not--I repeat--DO NOT think it's a two-way street: it might never be "reciprocated" in return. Just because you're nice &/or you have "good intentions", don't believe the other person has those same intentions. People have a funny way of "interpreting" what they hear, & a way of "twisting things around" to their advantage to make them look good in the eyes of others, but "dispel" you in the eyes of the beholder. Therefore, ALWAYS be the "better" person...Be NICE...Be HAPPY...& you, my friend, will ALWAYS have INNER PEACE :)

# The THREE "Periods" of Life (or, just another "hockey analogy" :) ...

*40ᵗʰ Birthday party cake of Ty for Melinda, 2010*

In order to stay "glued" together in life, I feel you have to separate things into three "periods to analyze you life...just like a hockey game.

There's different "stages" for everyone & there's so many things I'd like to make better. I'd like to share with you now some ideas that I feel would make the people of this wonderful planet much happier, much more positive—at least here in the United States:

1. We need to either raise the age to enlist in the armed forces to 21 &/or the right to vote to 21…my reasoning: if you have to wait until your 21 in order to legally have an alcoholic beverage, then why should you be sent to protect your country & have the unfortunate possibility of having your life end before your 21. I don't get that—make the age the same across the board.

2. I look at things in stages of 20 year periods…I feel at age 60, you should be able to retire & be able to enjoy at least 20-30 years of your life. Why don't we lower the eligible retirement age to 60…I think many people would rejoice over this. In my view, Social Security & Individual Retirement Accounts are dwindling over time because people can't really enjoy the life savings they've accumulated because they're working well into their 70's now—working until a sickness slows them down, or they eventually pass away altogether.

3. **THE** thing I always remind my children & my players that I coach is that we're all only here for a limited time. The earth has been around millions of years, but most of us are fortunate

if we can be here for 100 years! Think about it—look at my "analogy" again, for the 20 year stages:

From Birth until 20—the "formulative" years, where you grow into a man, or woman

From 20 until 40—the "feeling out" years, where you establish yourself

From 40 until 60—the "middle ground" years, where you nurture yourself & your surroundings

From 60 until 80—the "golden age" years, where you enjoy & reflect, & have "you" time

Once you hit 80, I feel you've lived a pretty long life—be fortunate & thank God for blessing you to be around for that mount of time. I cherish every day, every moment I can spend with my son & daughter, & try my best to make it count.

# Modern-day "Mantra's" for LIFE...

*Father's Day, 2016*

As you'll see throughout "Glue", I have many "thoughts" that I express w/conviction, w/vigor, but they're ALL from my heart, my gut & my soul. The following 10 "Mantra's" are life views that I try to live by each day: I remind myself of these every waking moment to take heed in them, & to strive to live my life these ways ALWAYS...

1. Always, **Find the "Gray":** not every day will always be totally Black and/or White, therefore you need to find the Gray in

between the two. "Never get too up, never get too down" is the philosophy to believe in…always take the good with the bad, & stay grounded.

2. It's best to **convey your thoughts in person**. Some things in life are not meant to be stated in a text message, an e-mail message, a phone call, & a written note and/or letter. It's best when it's done face-to-face. I think it's the most positive way to reinforce to others how much you really care & it's more personal, & heartfelt.

3. **Do not be taken advantage of in life**: treat each other with respect & dignity…as the bible says "do unto others as they have done unto you". Wouldn't you rather be nice to one another than be mean, or ornery? I'm not trying to "sugarcoat" anything here: I'm just saying it pays to be good to each other in life—& be happy!

4. EVERYONE should be a **"free thinker"**: form your own opinions, thoughts & goals—NO ONE should force their beliefs on anyone. BE YOU…"Believe In Yourself" & take your own initiative ALWAYS.

5. Be a **"team player"** when involved in groups (i.e. employment, team sports): yearn to be selfless, not selfish.

6. **Ideas are "visions imbedded in our souls".** Always think "pro"gressively, not "re"gressively to strive to make things better & improve upon what's already available w/new, "fresh" thoughts.

7. **Be the "glue"** that keeps people & holds life experiences together. Life is like the pieces of a puzzle: each piece has to fit just right to make it complete, one whole, solid structure...& it takes the "glue" to keep it together.

8. Life today is more about **"integrity"** than anything else. The way you conduct yourself, & the way you treat others speaks volumes of what a person's character is—& ALWAYS show respect for EVERYTHING God has created...

9. **The way we're "perceived" rules our thoughts: but don't EVER let it consume you.** There's something inside all of us, holding us back, holding us from being true, from being our real selves...our MIND. Only you can overcome this thought "process"—no one else.

10. **ALWAYS BE REAL**...I'm not perfect: I'm human...I'll always do my best & IF I don't do well, I take responsibility...I love life...I DO NOT judge & I accept everyone for who they are... Be "open": Wear your "heart on your sleeve", & Don't "hide your feelings".

# Coaching IS Life...

2016 MOIHA JV Champs

2013 MOIHA Jr. High Champs

2012 MOIHA Jr. High Champs

_**Sports are a reflection of life**_...Coaching is my passion...& Hockey is my love. It's the bonds, the relationships, & the comraderie of the players, coaches & parents that fills my spirit. With me, it isn't always about winning...it's about doing your best, coming together as a unit, & making "family" memories. Sometimes, that's what it takes to make a great team, no matter the won/loss record. I'm so honored to have played, coached & reffed sports...but there's nothing like what I've been surrounded by in hockey—especially the 2 Jr. High State Championship teams ('12 & '13) I've coached, & the Jr. Varsity team of 2016 that recently won the State Championship. I've also been on the losing side as well, but those teams were so different in personnel & personality. It always amazes me where a team can take themselves when they play as "one whole" & "believe".

A philosophy of mine in coaching players--especially youngsters--is their well-being, &/or "future" is more important to me than anything else. Life is not always about wins & losses...it's about becoming an adult, becoming one, becoming whole--as a person. How you shape yourself into what you eventually will become is more important to me. When you think about it, we're all players in the "game of life'" &--in my eyes--it's more important to be a winner in life, than a winner on the sports playing field. Don't get me wrong: it's important to do your best in a game, but it's more important to be the best person you can be to others, whether as a sibling, a parent, a spouse, a teacher/mentor, or--especially--as a friend to others. ALWAYS set a good example...& ALWAYS, "Win w/class, Lose w/class".

Another philosophy I strongly believe in when coaching younger people is the **'KISS Principle'—Keep It Simple System**. I also try to stress is how it's more mental than physical most of the time: don't try to "over-think" & "react" more to things—it's more about instincts than anything. Therefore, there's 5 things I try to instill at each & every practice, or before, during, or after EVERY game:

- Keep things simple, keep things fun
- Every player has a role on the team, no matter how experienced they are
- **Coaches coach, players play, parents parent...**
- ALWAYS be on the same page as the players, & their families
- "Win w/class, lose w/class"

In sports--& in everyday life--**Adversity** is something else we all go through. Sometimes, it's a good thing, in order to keep you grounded & you realize how bad you have to work at something in order to achieve & attain your goals. There are certain scenarios we take for granted at times & that's why you need to be thankful for the good (i.e.

winning, an excellent day) when you also have to go through the bad (i.e. losing, a tough day). One of my all-time "Coach Gregism's" is this: **From Adversity, one builds Courage, Confidence & Character**...it's something you learn & must retain. Adversity also breeds **Perseverance**: you can overcome anything in life once you **BELIEVE**--it's more mental than physical the majority of the time too. Remember **3 other things** & you'll always prosper & overcome anything: "Keep the **FAITH**, **HOPE** for the best, **BE**lieve in **YOU**rself". IF you live out ALL of these "aspects" in life, you'll never fail—& you'll ALWAYS "Be Your Best".

One thing about today's society is that's come to the forefront is the emphasis of **athletes as role models.** One of the best quotes I've ever heard was by NBA Hall of Famer, Charles Barkley: "I'm not a role model—I shouldn't be your kids role model...the parents need to be". I couldn't agree more. Parents nowadays also put too much emphasis on winning & living "their" dreams through their children. Therefore, the biggest game of all is "LIFE"—I care more about what happens to my players & families than what actually transpires during the actual games...& ALL of us--especially parents--must stress this principle daily.

Another sports "concept" that's come to fruition over time is **Parity** has been created in the professional leagues, due to salary caps, in order to make a "level playing field" for all teams. I feel the same type of thing has to be created for ALL forms of children's sports. Then again, you do have A, B, C, &/or 'Tiers' in certain team sports &--as I stated--its good to have ALL "like" competition on the same level in order to give the players & teams a fair chance.

However, in today's ways of "finding an edge" in EVERYTHING, there have become too many **'select' sports teams** for kids—it's too costly for parents too—plus there's not enough opportunities for everyone to play. I feel every child deserves to play something—everyone deserves a role on a team & have access to play. When it comes to individual sports though, it's all on you. Team sports must be played "collectively" together—if not, it ruins the "whole" of the team concept. There's also a need for **'learn to play'** opportunities for all ages—not just children, but adults too....& just because you play a 'select' sport, it doesn't mean you're going to have a huge advantage in making high school team(s), or even playing in college. It's not fair to restrict the kids on what they can & cannot do: let them enjoy a variety of sports & events, & let them make their own choices when it comes to anything they partake in life.

One thought that I always instill into my players minds is to always use **"vision"**...whether it's in sports, or life in general, you've got to use your mind, your imagination, like a "projector on a big screen". I can break it down as a player, a coach, a father & a human being—they're part of my "analogies of 4" to convey what I'm saying to others.

**Peripheral vision is the most important type of vision in my eyes too...look** straight ahead, look out of the sides of your eyes to the left & right. All types of vision help propel your focus & it puts the "big picture" into perspective a well...."don't take your eye off of the prize" (hand/eye coordination), or "don't lose sight of the puck" (watch it into the glove, especially if you're a Goalie) are the two I stress the most.

A "pet peeve" of mine in life, sports & coaching, is being **"Consistently Inconsistent"**...it can apply to many things in athletics, especially officiating. In my eyes, it doesn't matter if it's "pee-wee", high school, college, or professional sports, if you put people in charge of judging what's "fair" & what's foul, it's not fool proof, or ever— EVER—perfect. You're dealing with human beings & they're relying on "the naked eye" to make the appropriate call. The majority of the time, officials do get it right. HOWEVER, mistakes will happen—it's a matter of admitting they're wrong if they blew the call—sometimes they will & I respect that. It's the one's that are bull-headed, stubborn & "I'm never wrong because I'm always right" that ruin it for everyone else. I've officiated sports & it can be a 'thankless' job. The thing is people will respect you more when you're right & can substantiate when you're wrong & you admit it. You're human, we're all human: it happens.

As a Hockey Coach, I'm adamant w/my Goalies about making the save, rather than worrying about their **"technique"**. As I always say, "keep things simple & don't overthink"--& that's my "mantra" on almost EVERYTHING now. Whether it's sports, managing my life, my health & well being--they're ALL separate issues here, but I'm trying to use "common sense" approach to everything. So, when it comes to Goaltending in Roller Hockey, this is my "philosophy"...tell yourself "nothing will get by me", but allow yourself to be human. IF you make 2-3 mistakes a period & you allow 4-6 goals, HOPEFULLY, your team will score at least 5-7 goals to seal the Win (In Ice, 1 Goal per Period, 3 per game...score 4 or more & you usually Win). The Goalie MUST remember they're the "last line of defense": you have to have everyone's back, but they have to perform in front of you as well. You can't do it alone: you must play as a team to succeed.

Ask yourself this question: **"what motivates you most?"** Whether it's a sports event, or a life experience, it can be broken down in one of 3 manners...

1. **Playing the "percentages".** It's ironic how--in sports--a .500 season, or better, is looked upon as a success in many circles, but a failure if you're well below that mark. However, in academics, if you score below 80%, it's mainly considered "average". If you're just average in life, you'll probably never flourish, or see your true potential, because there's so many that just "get by" & are average, rather than always trying their best to succeed.

My philosophy: try your best to be "above average" 80-90%, or "exceptional" 90-100%...you'll actually get ahead in life & hopefully fulfill your potential IF you strive for this mark.

2. **PLAYING to win vs. EXPECTING to win**: there's a MAJOR difference. You must never be ungrateful &/or under-estimate your opponent. On paper, some teams look better than others... however, if you don't play w/heart & soul, or work hard, then "hard work will always prevail over talent that doesn't work hard". Therefore, ALWAYS be respectful & do your best.

3. **Bulletin Board Material**": Be VERY careful what you say, Be VERY careful what you wish, because "karma" has a way of biting you in the ass, especially when you don't stay "humble". Don't give your competition any "motivation" to make them more "inspired" to win, or beat your butt to a pulp...you're only asking for it, if you do.

What I'm stating is **"stay motivated & follow through"**. You cannot win, or succeed, on talent alone: you have to want 'it'. Without hard work and a lack of 'chemistry' around you, it's tough to do it all alone...& Cohesiveness" is the essential key.

"**Leadership**" comes from earning the respect of others, and promoting a positive atmosphere under all circumstances...you are not entitled to be a leader: you're born with the trait, where you work hard to attain it, and--in the end--you earn it. "**Leading by example**" in sports & life is essential too. I remember once, before a game started that I was coaching, I used this analogy on my team, "If so-&-so was going to jump off a bridge, would you follow, or what would you do?" Believe it or not, I received 3 different answers, from 3 different players:

1. "How high's the bridge?"

2. "Is there water underneath the bridge?"

3. "Is there a rope nearby to throw to him to catch & we'll pull him back up?"

...isn't it interesting to see how one question can have so many interpretations, & a variety of answers? That, my friend, is what life's all about: **making the right choices**...

As you can tell, coaching hockey is an important aspect of my life--probably THE thing that motivates me to be my best EVERY day. Back in 2009--when I first started coaching in MOIHA--I was told that we (Parkway & P-South) were "in over our heads", we had "no clue what we're doing"...the best was "no one in West County St. Louis can compete on this level &/or EVER win a Championship". Here we are, in 2016--7seasons later--& we've won 3 State Championships, & competed in the playoffs EVERY season w/ALL of our teams...not too shabby. Therefore--as a player, parent, ref, or coach—even though I/we have been put down, I ALWAYS stress to EVERYONE to treat your opponents w/respect...don't think you're bigger & better than them &/or the game itself. Stay humble & you'll be "respected" by everyone ALWAYS.

# "From A Player's & Parent's "Perspective"...

Colin in his "element"

**"The Rink is MY Sanctuary"**, whether it's roller, ice, or the Scottrade Center...it's my "happy place". If there's one atmosphere where I feel a connection with others, where I feel accepted & "glued together, it's with my "hockey family". I came up with an idea as I was writing "Glue" to open up a chapter for the book...to let players & parents from the hockey family to share their thoughts of how they feel about the sport of hockey, & my relationships with them in their family's hockey endeavors. Needless to say, this concept was well received...& I feel this might be the most "moving" part of "Glue", in my humble opinion. I feel that, sometimes, your audience is the author, instead of the actual writer...& I wanted to share my pen with them...

## The letter that "revived" me...

The best note I ever received in my entire life was from one of my players. It came at a time when I was suffering immensely from what I was going through after my surgery & the near-fatal Emergency Room visits in the Fall of 2015. I wanted to include it in its entirety, because it meant so much to me that an 18 year-old person thought this much of me, to "reach out" when I needed it most...

Dear Greg,

When I first met you as my middle school roller hockey coach, I thought that a coach was all you would be. Boy, was I wrong! After just the first practice, you told our team how much you would support us and have our backs no matter what the situation was, and you never let us down. You loved and cared for all of us as if we were family, and that's exactly what I have grown to be with you. You have become way more than a coach to me, and I thank you for this immensely!

I could not have asked for anything more from anyone but you. You always go above and beyond my expectations with everything that you do (especially those new roller hockey jerseys). Whenever I needed someone to talk to, I could always count on you for a long and meaningful conversation. I will always treasure the incredibly gracious words you expressed to me on my birthday. I do not feel more comfortable speaking with or being around any other adults than I do with you.

I always feel extremely welcomed by you, and always have a brightened day when I see you. I will always remember you for the positive impact you've had on my life, and I cannot thank you enough for everything that you do.

Thank you...

...This letter brought me "back to life": it made me want to Coach again, be a better person & Father, & it inspired me to "get myself right" & be "me" again...

## "Blessed"

It's truly a blessing to be a coach: I'm always humbled & honored to share my time on the rink with the players, & to also mentor them throughout life as well. "Blessings": that's what this message was from a player who has truly found his identity on the rink...& with our family...

"Greg... It's been an honor and a super great time to help practice with the C and JV team: I've always been supportive to help practice. I'm truly blessed to have this opportunity to play this great sport with such great teammates, and most of all, the best coach I could ever ask for: always happy, and super energetic when we play defense, and score goals...and especially win championships--the looks on your face puts smiles on everyone else's face. You're easily the best coach I have ever had, and you will always be my favorite coach, and one of the most important people in my life that I look up to...especially being my 2nd father, and I thank you, and you guys, for being my second family. I'm so blessed that I have made friends with your son, and met all of you. You guys have taught me so much, and have made me a special, and different person. I probably wouldn't even be playing hockey if it wasn't for your son. I just want to say thank you so much, and I hope I get to come home soon: I love you all."

Many things have moved me to tears over the years...it's those "happy" tears that I retain the most, such as what the young man wrote above. But there's others who have bought into the "less is more" approach, as I have, in sharing their thoughts. Some great quotes some parents & players have come up with were very simple, but very inspiring & from the heart...

- Words cannot describe how thankful I am to have you in my life...
- You're my best friend, Coach Greg...
- It's an unreal experience helping you behind the bench— you truly are the best...
- Never has one man done so much for so many boys...
- My boys always have a great time playing for you & the program. You know how much playing hockey has made a difference in my boys' lives, & I have you to thank!
- ***One of my players had this analogy that he wanted to share...*** The way a team plays as a whole determines its success. You may have the greatest bunch of individual stars in the world, but if they don't play together, the club isn't worth a dime." In other words, a team might look great on paper, and in warm-ups, but they must ultimately play the game...and anything can happen.
- Greg is a Coach with Character who isn't afraid to show it all the time for the players he coaches: thank you!

- The Parkway South Roller Hockey families thank you for always giving 100% & for just being you--it's a privilege to play for you...

- Greg, you have hands down helped me through life more than anyone else. You're the strongest man I've ever met...

## "Coach Greg's IMPACT"

I met another young man at the beginning of 2008, when he was in 4th Grade & just learning to play hockey. He played w/my son from day one, ALL the way up until this past Spring, his Senior season. Needless to say, we BOTH made a huge impact on each other's lives...& this is what he submitted to me in late July...

What goes on in an eleven year-old kid's head when he's picking up a new sport for the very first time? Anticipation? Excitement? Fear of making a fool out of yourself? For me, all three of these were present prior to my first day of heading into being a hockey player, but mostly the fear of embarrassment. "Will the coach like me?", I thought to myself. The second I met my coach, the fear was no more. You know those type of people you meet in the world and just think to yourself, "oh year, we're gonna get along", that's what this was—an immediate bond.

Throughout my first season of hockey, I enjoyed the season more than I can imagine. A trio was combined with a tightly knit group of my coach's son, and a kid we called "the Terrier". Looking down the road of memory lane, these three did some damage together with the help of Greg.

In my first year as a junior high student, Greg decided to conduct a team full of Parkway related students to participate in the "MOIHA" league A rough season would be an understatement regarding that year. We failed to win a single game that season and faced a plethora of adversity. None of the players would give up on Coach Greg that following season. We couldn't because we knew he would do whatever he could to make us a better team next year. He would very much do so, leading our team to our first winning record. That year we were knocked out in the state semifinals, leaving some unfinished business on our platter for our final season as teammates for our Junior High careers.

In the midst of our season I will never forget, I was taken off the roster due to some disagreements with an Assistant Coach. I knew my team would be unable to take home the hardware without me in the lineup, and neither did Greg. No matter the sport, that's what each player wants from their coach. They want confidence in their players and that's exactly what Coach Greg did, as he reinstated me for the playoffs. In a 2-2 game in the dying minutes of the State Finals, I hopped off the bench in the dying minutes of the game, with a little under a minute to go. As the puck was carried into the zone by former teammate ("Scooter"), I headed to the net with a head of speed to open up for a pass. Scooter would place a perfect pass on my blade, avoiding the defender. It was just me, and the Goalie now and I wouldn't miss… The next thing I remembered was being mauled by Scooter to celebrate the goal, then looking up at the clock and reading .16 seconds to go. Boom! STATE CHAMPIONS! I will never forget that goal nor the reason it happened: Greg gave me another chance.

Without the help of Greg as a person and a coach, I would never be able to say I served as an Assistant Captain for the 7th Ranked Ice Hockey team in Mid-State Hockey. Without the help of Greg, I wouldn't have tallied 41 points in the highest Tier of MOIHA. Without Greg, I wouldn't have formed the unforgettable friendships with every teammate I wore the same jersey as with him as Coach. Most importantly, I would not have grown into the young man I am to this day without his help. He grew my character as a person, and love for the game of hockey. How much he gives and goes through with his players is something special. Whether you're a member of the AAA Blues, or just trying out hockey for the very first time (like I did), Greg will give you a shot.

Outside of the game of hockey, Greg was always there for me. When I was having trouble regarding anything, he'd listen to me and help me out. Him and his family served as a second family for me. His home was a second home. It's sad that I will never play another hockey game for him, but I am truly very blessed that I will stay in touch with him and his family the rest of his life. There are special people out in this world...luckily for me, I was able to meet one my first day of hockey.

As I typed this up to put into the "Glue" manuscript, by the time I was on Page 2, tears were streaming down my cheeks, as I realized how much our friendship meant to each other through the years. He came to our house the day before he left for college, had dinner w/us & visited... as he drove away, he rolled down his window & said, "Greg...think of this as your first-born son is leaving for college...as you say: 'it's all good'...". As I walked back into my house, I teared up, but didn't break down...why, you ask? Because I know we will always have each other's backs--I will always be there for him, & he'll be there for me as well...

## "Full Circle"

In life, sometimes things go "full circle", & you re-unite with someone from your past, whom you never knew you had already made an impact on...

I was four when we moved into our new house. The house was across the street from the neighborhood park. Moving into a new neighborhood, especially at a young age, I didn't know anyone. My family has always been a hockey family, so when I saw people practicing at the park, I would always grab my stick & go over to play, not knowing that one day, I would meet the man who would change my life had just occurred. Fast forward 7 years, I'm winning a JV Roller Hockey State Championship with him as Head Coach.

Greg has not only impacted my hockey career, but also my personal life. He has gone to bat for me countless times: he is truly selfless. From a hockey standpoint, if Greg is on the bench, you know your team is already far superior to the other, just by coaching alone. He also impacted my life personally when he took me in, and made me a part of his "hockey family". If anyone deserves this book, it's Greg--he gives so much to us (the players), he deserves something back.

...This young man has an incredible future in front of him & I'm so proud of him--always...

## What is "SUCCESS"?

My son wrote the following for a paper in his College Comp class. He asked me to help edit it for him, but to read it out loud...little did

I know, by the time I got to the second page, I realized "who" he was talking about...

What determines success in life? Is it a person's character? If they are a great, loyal, and honest person, or someone who doesn't care for too many people, but put in heart, dedication, and determination, then they will be successful. Now, success is not gifted to you on a silver platter. I once heard someone say, "If you want to succeed as bad as you want to breathe, then you will be successful". I have always agreed with this statement because—nowadays—no one wants to work towards anything.

If someone is playing a sport and they are the best on the team at their specific position, they expect that spot to be handed to them. What should happen is that spot should not be gifted because of skill, it should be earned through heart, dedication, and determination. People who work harder in the classroom, at their work, and in athletics, tend to be the people who succeed later on in life...

For example, there is someone that I know pretty well who is a single child, who grew up with divorced parents--this person hasn't had the easiest life. They have seen things and heard things no one should have to bear. They have had many injuries throughout their life, which hindered their success in athletics during their younger years, and has given everything they have for the people they love, just to have it all turn up short of success. But, in order to succeed, you must have determination, and heart. And this person has just that. This person wanted to succeed as bad as they wanted to breathe. This person has taken the word "success" and has become the definition of it. This person has coached four teams to State Championships, and won three of them. This person has been recruited to coach at the college level instead of coaching middle school, and high school students. This person has also had a dream of writing their own book, but thought it was just a dream. But this person put in heart, dedication, and determination into this dream, and they have just signed a three book contract with a publisher. This dream is success. This person had all the key components to achieve anything they wanted and he did it. This person had heart, dedication, and determination. That is what I call success…

…My son's paper was about me: I absolutely sobbed, hugged him, & told him, "I love you son: that was the most incredible thing you've ever done for me—I'm forever honored & humbled to be your Father…" I guess you could say that my son "gets it" when it comes to life…THIS was my proudest moment ever as his Father.

## "Two-Way Street"

Sometimes, in life, we meet someone that comes into our lives that makes us a better person. For me, it's always been a two-way street, where the player makes just as much of an impact on me, as I have on them...

Back in February of 2013, my son was a freshman. He had begun playing for Parkway when he was in 7th Grade. He had played baseball since he was in preschool &--like "The Wizard", Ozzie Smith--he was a defensive specialist. One of his first coaches called him "Hoover" because he sucked up every ball hit his way. Even as early as first grade, his glove stood out. Normally, you would play the tallest kid at first base because he has the longest reach. My son, being the smallest kid on his team, was the least likely candidate. By the end of his first year, he was the first basemen because he was the kid that always caught the ball.

Starting at that time, my son's daily ritual was the same... I would come home from work, and he would be waiting for me in the driveway with his glove and ball. He practiced catching everyday, and it showed throughout his grade school years. Every team my son played for, he had the best glove on the team. He always wanted to play hockey too, but there weren't many opportunities to play. When my son was real young, I still played in Men's recreation leagues, and he would come watch. I always meant to find a league for him to join, but it took until 7th grade before I finally got him into the Parkway organization. Most of the kids had been playing for a long time, and were far ahead of my son in skating, and stick handling.

When it came time to pick between the two sports his Freshman year at South, it seemed obvious to pick baseball. My son would have loved to have played both, but, because the league's both played in the Spring, that wasn't possible. He had been working out in the gym twice a week for 3 months with the baseball team. Then, we were asked to volunteer to fix up the field in the Spring. Then came the fundraiser: we were asked to fill a $200 table for trivia, and donate a prize, so I put together a really cool basket with World War 2 books, pictures, and memorabilia that was probably worth $200. I remember that after my son told you he was trying out for baseball, and he wouldn't be able to play hockey, you still offered to keep a spot open for him, just in case. The week of baseball tryouts, it snowed, and the boys never made it outside to the baseball field. My son's glove was only shown on the gym floor, where he successfully fielded 20 out of 20 balls. At the end of the week, him and his buddy (who rode together to tryouts) were in the locker room waiting to find out about the team. The coached informed my son that he was being cut, and he had to leave the locker room. Because his friend--who my son was every bit as good as he was--made the team, my son had to wait there for him. I can only imagine how tough that had to be hearing the other boys celebrate making the team, as my son sat out in the hall. He came home very sad and defeated.

A couple days later, his mom and I broke the news to him that we were getting a divorce. None of our kids took this news very well, but it seemed to hurt my son a lot. He has always been a very loving, caring, and sensitive person.

This is when you stepped in, Greg...

God always seems to put the right people in the right place just at the time they are needed. Though my son's baseball coach did not see the value in a small kid with a big heart, you seemed very happy to have him as part of your hockey team. This saved my son in so many ways. It gave him back his confidence, and his self-esteem. He was very proud to wear anything that said "Parkway Hockey". A few weeks later, my son told me he was picked to be the Captain of the team. He wore that Jersey with the "C" with a lot of pride. Four years later, all we could think was, "Thank God that baseball coach was stupid enough to cut him". Playing hockey for you, and Parkway, was the highlight of his high school years. I know he will always look back, and miss those days. I thank you for believing in him, and I thank God for bringing you into his life.

Again, as I typed this up, I couldn't help but cry, because of the bond we had created as player & coach...it made me feel that I had a "purpose" in life--& I thank God he walked into my life, just as much as his father thanked me for being there for him.

## Lifetime "Bond"

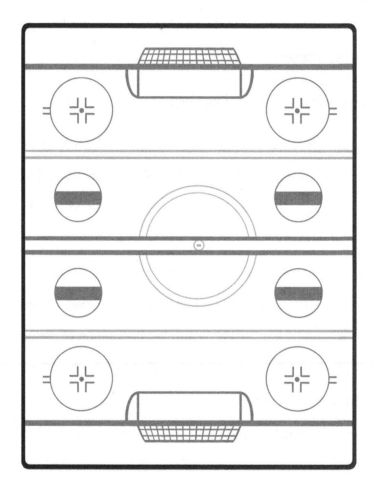

Illustration by Ryan Litteken

In your life, you meet someone, or a group of people, that you automatically form a friendship with that will last forever, from the moment you say "hello". You complete each other's thoughts, you think exactly alike--they're like your "twin". I've had many friendships like this, but THIS one "takes the cake"...& it is the very last thought I put in "Glue"...

This is a story about one of the greatest people I have ever had the chance to know. First, let me tell you about me. I am a mother of 3 amazing boys, & I am also a Registered Nurse. I am a loud, passionate, stubborn German girl that loves with my whole heart. I think that is why Greg and I were meant to be in each other's lives--a truly wonderful spirit with a heart of gold.

Greg and I became friends because our son and daughter are in the same grade at the same school. We had a lot in common, and--as time went on--I realized that he valued the same things I do: love, family, friendships, caring for others, & helping in any way he can. I pride myself on the same qualities...but Greg takes them to another level.

I came to know this first hand as years went by. What really made me come to know the goodness of Greg's soul, however, was in July of 2015, when I almost died. I had become very depressed after the death of my father, and the end of my 13-year marriage. Then came the biggest blow of all: I lost my job after 16 years of service to others as a nurse. I felt like nothing... I had nothing. Not even my kids were enough to make me want to live, so I basically drank to numb the pain... I drank until it almost killed me. I spent 28 days in the hospital...my family treated me like a loser...my friends started dropping out of my life. Greg, and his family, stepped in. Greg never made me feel like I was worthless, never made me feel ashamed, nor embarrassed. Greg was always there to lend an ear or a helping hand: he never judged me for being weak, because Greg never judges anyone--that's just Greg.

As time went on, and I went through my recovery process, Greg always gave me support...just a quick note, or a card, to brighten my day. Greg also puts everyone ahead of himself always. This proved to not be the best thing for Greg, however, when I learned that he was having great struggles of his own...

Now, it was time for Greg to need help...& helpers don't like to be helped...

As Greg struggled through a deep depression of his own, he began to have health issues: SERIOUS health issues. I made sure I tried to be available to help as much as possible. Greg and I would have long talks... I know they not only helped him, but also helped me. Greg would apologize for being a "burden", &--even though I told him constantly that I was there to help him--he felt like he should be doing the helping, not the other way around. Then, there came a point with Greg that I knew he needed some tough love... I knew because I am him...and he is me. In the end, the only person that can help you...is YOU. As difficult as it was, I feel like I gave Greg what he needed at the time: the strength to see his way out of the darkness. Greg came out so much better on the other side, as I always knew he would. He is absolutely one of the strongest people I know.

Greg is also a hockey coach. He took interest in my oldest son playing for him. Now, I got to see the coaching side of this man I call "the bestest"...& that word does not even do him justice. Greg coaches with such heart, & he loves his "hockey family", which he immediately adopted us right into. He has taught my son humility, respect, and a passion for the game that no one else I know has, or could. My son has become a second son to Greg, & I am so grateful that he is such an incredible man to look up to, and gain values from.

To say that Greg has a heart of gold is an understatement. He tells me frequently how "I saved him"...but, he doesn't realize how much he saved me. Greg shined his light into my dark hole, and helped show me the way out. He helped me feel like a confident nurse again when I felt like a huge failure. Greg helped show me what true friendship means, & I feel as though I could never say "thank you" enough for all he is to me, and my three sons.

In my eyes, Greg is "Glue". He is the Glue that puts people back together, takes their broken pieces, and helps put them back together, even though he, himself, is broken. "Pay it forward" is one of my favorite phrases in life, & I try to emulate this in my home life, as well as my professional career. Greg pays it forward in everything he does: he is "Glue".

God brings people into your life when you need them the most. You may not always realize it at first, but when you open your heart to others, you may find that you get more from them than you could possibly give back. So sit back, relax, and let life happen...because you never know who your "Glue" might be.

When I first received this letter & read it, I sobbed: I cried like a baby. I never fully realized the impact & inspiration that I had on my friend & her three sons...& vice-versa. She's become my best friend & her son's are very special young man. I thank God each day for bringing them into my life, & me into theirs, & ALL of the players I've ever coached for that matter. THIS message is what being "Glue" is all about: **life can be a puzzle of sorts**, but having the "Glue" to bring people together, keep people together, & be there for each other--ALWAYS--that's what life is...

Throughout my years in coaching, I've always promoted a "**family first**" atmosphere. Yes, players play, coaches coach, parents parent. However, my philosophy is that a team is much like your family, and everyone has a purpose, and serves a role within the "sum of its parts". You might not always get along, but you respect one another, you play for one another, and become one collective whole. And when one person within the group needs something--whether it's a player, parent, or coach--we support one another...and you can always come to me to open up. Furthermore, I'm more concerned about the game of life, and what happens off the rink, than what actually transpires during the games. That's why I profess "hockey family" to anyone, and everyone that's ever been a part of our Parkway, Parkway South, &--NOW--St. Louis Community College Roller Hockey programs.

# ** Coming Unglued AGAIN…

# but Not by Design **

I received a wake-up call--TWICE--in the Fall of 2015. I was experiencing my third back surgery within three years time--& this procedure was to correct the first one I ever had done on my neck/upper back & spine section. Little did I know I was going to have complications this time in recovering…not from the actual surgery, but from the medicine "mix-ups" my mind & body would go through. Therefore, the main reason I FINALLY decided to finish "Glue" was I became "unglued" again…but not by design. At age 49, you realize what matters most in life, & I didn't want to live w/any regrets. Therefore, I stopped procrastinating & finished what I started back in 2009. When you almost die twice within a 2-week time-frame, you re-evaluate yourself, your life, & decide what takes priority.

With ALL of the people that had judged me in years past, I knew they would again, since I became unglued AGAIN. Furthermore, there would probably be a lot more people this time around as well. It's mainly a small "minority" of people that live within the area I reside that feel this way about me, but the positive peeps outweigh the nay-sayers by a landslide. It's too bad they don't know "the real me", but that's life. All I know is this…IF I can make it through what I experienced for that 6-week period (October 29, 2015, until December 10, 2015), I can make it through ANYTHING & EVERYTHING life throws at me…

When you almost die twice within a two-week time frame, you really re-evaluate your life, & the purpose of why we're all here. The worst part is not remembering what transpired two weeks before, & two weeks after the surgery…a 6-week fog, or—as I call it—6 weeks of pure hell. Having 3 back surgeries within 3 years time can take it's toll too…but, little did I know that my 3rd surgery—one to repair discrepancies with the first one I had—would take such an awful turn. EVERYTHING that happened this time coming "un-glued" wasn't by choice…it was medicine mixes gone wrong that cause me to have an extreme anxiety attack—nothing like I ever experienced in my life previously—and the other put me into diabetic shock. The fear of feeling that your heart was about to explode, coinciding with your brain feeling it was about to pop, culminating two weeks later by your blood sugars dropping to dangerous levels to the point of shaking & extreme cold, it truly wakes you up. You ask yourself, "Can I ever have surgery again?"...then again, you should say, "Why did this ever happen to me?".

I also ended up having a second "stint" in Outpatient Therapy, due to the Anxiety & PanicAttacks ALL of the "med-mixes gone wrong" created. However, as positive as my experience was in '08, it did not go as well as the first time: it was "counter-productive" in a sense...I didn't have that "connection" with the staff as I did the first time around. I will admit, I made 3 friends for life this time around though, as they inspired me, as much as I inspired them, each day in our group sessions. The one thing that came out "positive from a negative": I CAN DO THIS...& I can get better, & be better on My Own...on My Terms.

I'm fortunate enough that the hospital staff, where I had the surgery, took great care of me...to the point that I actually met with the President of the Hospital & the Director of Nursing, to discuss what I experienced. They were so moved by what happened that they asked me to be part of a training video for the hospital employees, which expounded on what I endured after my surgery & those 6 weeks of utter hell I went through. It's amazing to know that—in this day & age—there are still many people that are compassionate about the human "spirit", & they are actually looking out for your best interest, & the goal that you'll go on to live a full & productive life. For this, I am forever indebted to this privately owned hospital in the St. Louis area, their Doctors & staff, the ER department, &--especially--4 nurses that guided me through…one in particular that personally helped me through the extreme reactions of the med mixes. God is good, especially Nurses…they're probably the most kind hearted, compassionate souls that exists on this planet…what they experience, what they endure— they are THE "Glue" of the Medical world.

With all of the good &/or great things I've experienced in my life, I've also had a plethora of bad vibes, rough times & Demons. You realize in life that you ALWAYS have to find that Gray lining, between the Black & the White…& sometimes, things that happen are not really your fault & are out of your control. That's where you find the inner strength to overcome anything & everything, plus you find out "who" will be there to support you & help you out as well. The first thing you must do when facing a dilemma…help yourself, because no one else can--you have to do it…

Even though I'm a totally different person from back in the Summer of '08, some people have 'whispered' that I've never been the same &-- this time around-- "I'm worse". They can't tell me face-to-face, but that's OK. Actually—I'm not the same & I wouldn't want to be. I think I'm a better person for it & I cannot lie to myself and/or others. People had termed me as "Broken & Damaged", in the past, which I understand somewhat, but now, I'm "Mentally Challenged" this time around? WOW! I pleaded to God, "why do people hurt one another without knowing the **"Facts vs. Perception'?"** & there's **"no responsibilities for their actions" from others can be "the norm"** sometimes. But I do find solace in this thought: I love ALL of the kids I've ever coached, in the past & now—they've always accepted me, respected me & are grateful for whatever I've tried to do for them. I'm more concerned about their futures, & their children & their children's children.

We all should realize something else... No one is perfect: we all make mistakes. As long as we learn from them, correct them, & move on, all is well. However, when the same mistake(s) are being made over & over again, that can become a problem. It's almost like an addiction that you cannot break...& then it becomes habitual. Live & learn, as I say...but don't repeat it over & over, because--IF you do--it can consume you & break you down. Rise up & overcome what the mistake &/or problem is: you'll be better off in the end.

One thing that really bothered me throughout this experience is that I ultimately had to straighten out my medications & taking pills. It made me a person that I'm really not, & that weighs on me constantly, more so mentally than physically. For years, I've felt "over medicated" at times, due to my health issues. It's not fun to constantly take pain meds, just to feel better & get through the day. Honestly, some days, I feel so "incoherent" that all I want to do is sleep. But I finally "broke through the cycle". However, I'm convinced that America is completely **"over-medicated"**. There seems to be a TV commercial on ever 15 minutes promoting this, or that, & how it will help you, but it contains a plethora of side effects that will affect everything else inside our body. What a shame: is this what we've become--just like taking one step forward, but a triple-jump backwards.

Another thing I used to have was a great memory...just like an Elephant, the ones who "never forget". I remember most everything that has happened every day in my life...all it takes is a "trigger" to bring back a vivid memory, whether good or bad. It's a blessing, it's a curse, but I'm glad it's ingrained in me. However, with the memory loss I suffered after the medicine mix complications from this surgery in October, 2015, there comes a feeling of not knowing what you once were: who you know, what you did—many things are altered. But that's ok, especially if some things that happened were traumatic--it's better off not knowing exactly what you endured. What's also affected is your "processing speed": you cannot answer as quickly as you once did, & things are in "slow-mo" . It's tough to put a finger on it, but maybe it's in your best interest(s) to slow down, instead of living so fast too. Within time, I became more focused on everyday tasks & activities, that my memory did come back for the most part—minus that six week period.

One thing that has become better though: my focus--it's actually amazing now. I do firmly believe that after what I endured through those six weeks of my life, I'm not sure I can ever be an "Elephant Thinker" again. All of the medication mixes affected me to the point that I cannot remember the surgery I had, the two Emergency Room visits where I almost died, or the Halloween & Thanksgiving holiday's w/my family: mostly everything from late-October until mid-December of 2015. Everything changed as the right medicine mix put me back on the path to being me again, and it has helped erase all of the traumatic events that happened in that time.

The medications made me a completely different person that I'm not proud of, & I still pray to God each day everyone around me forgives me, understands me & supports me for what I've been through, because it hasn't been easy. Actually, on Christmas Eve, I watched "The Bible" on the History Channel & it changed my "perspective" on life forever. It's amazing how Jesus, and his disciples, did so much good,

while others tried to tear them down. But they rose up, and persevered...
just like I have--&, in the end, good will always triumph over evil. All
glory & thanks be to God...

In conclusion, I'm so thankful to be alive, to be back as a positive
person, a mentor to many, & the friend everyone has always known
me as. I still hurt BOTH physically & mentally...& each day, there's a
moment where I feel like giving up & just "mailing it in". However, I
put on a brave face & tell myself to "never give up", because there's a
reason I'm still here--& we're ALL still here...it's God. He gives me the
inner strength to realize who I am & why I keep "pushing on"...because
I'm worth it. I know God ALWAYS forgives: I've forgiven myself as well,
&--from this point forward--nothing but positive vibes will expound
from me...& a clean, healthy, productive life, until I breathe my last
breathe here on planet earth. The outside of me is different as well, but
it's a much needed change for the better... I look younger, I look healthy,
I look happy & rested too. On the inside, I've never felt so calm in my
life, so reassured that I can handle anything & everything that comes
my way from this point forward. What a feeling it is to feel "good", to
feel "glued together" FINALLY.

# "...I want to 'Thank You'..."

Illustration by Blake Stone

In the words of of a song on Led Zeppelin's 2<sup>nd</sup> release, I want to "Thank You" for being a friend, for understanding what I've been through, for accepting me for who I am, for supporting me & for reading "Glue". Since this is my first foray in writing a book, there's 10 more things I'd like to share with all of you about me...

1.  IF **"Glue" & "The Book of Coach Gregism's" are well received by the masses, I'd like to become a full-time author.** I plan on releasing a 3rd book in late 2017, with the potential to write 2 more by 2020, & my eventual goal is to write a "trilogy & a prequel", similar to the "Lord of the Rings" series & "The Hobbit".

2.  There are 5 very important organizations that are near & dear to my heart, 3 of which are located the St. Louis Metro area that I'm a big advocate for. Please consider supporting the following when you're able:

    *   The "14" Fund (Cancer). In honor of former St. Louis Blue, Doug Wickenheiser, the Blues & the "Wick" family help raise funding to battle cancer & create awareness.

    *   Kaitlin Harris Foundation (Suicide Prevention). Three other St. Louis organizations that address suicide, and suicide prevention include Kids Under 21, Annie's Hope & the Megan Meier's Foundation.

    *   Stray Rescue of St. Louis (pets). Randy Grim, and his staff are remarkable in helping rehabilitate, and place dogs, and cats, in St. Louis metro area homes: consider a resume pet--they'll rescue you in return with their unconditional love & devotion.

- PTSD/Anxiety/Depression, and Diabetes treatment centers...we can ALL use support in life, especially when it comes to these medically diagnosed challenges.

- Stand For The Silent (Anti-bullying). Founded by Kirk Smalley in Oklahoma, this foundation helps those who have suffered through a loss, or self-esteem issues, due to bullying incidents: Kirk is a great man that does public speaking engagements as well.

3. I've lived in St. Louis my entire life...there are so many negatives vibes portrayed today in St. Louis, the U.S.—the whole world for that matter—that I will always stress the positive as much as I can. Especially for my hometown, St. Louis: it's in the center of the United States & it has so much to offer. My ultimate "dream" place to live would be in Colorado, or Canada (preferably Alberta, or Manitoba), in a log home, with a lake & mountains in the distance...

4. Besides coaching hockey, I've also coached baseball, basketball, soccer, & softball, plus I was in charge of running a sports program at our church for 4 years.

5. I LOVE SPORTS...& there's 5 sports events I'll always tune into on TV:

- St. Louis Blues Hockey, ANY NHL games, the Stanley Cup Playoffs, & major Hockey tourneys
- Major Soccer tourneys/games (i.e. World Cup, UEFA Cup, EURO Cup, Premier League)
- NCAA March Madness College Hoops
- NFL Sunday Night Football & Monday Night Football
- St. Louis Cardinals in the MLB Playoffs

6. My bucket list for life:

- Find a Cure for Cancer & other debilitating diseases...
- Develop better research for mental illnesses & help people understand what they entail...
- Colin, McKenna, ALL of the players that ever played for me, have happy & productive lives...
- ALL dogs & horses have a home...
- Blues win the Stanley Cup...

7. What "presses my buttons"--

1. The lack of respect people show one another these days...

2. People being untrustworthy...

3. Suffocating personalities...

4. Stupidity...

5. Talking about politics, or health insurance...

8. As I expounded on in an earlier chapter, music & I have a special connection, as it acts as my "therapist for my soul." Three releases that have "saved me" through the years are Rush "Exit...Stage Left", Pearl Jam "Ten" & Metallica's self-titled "Black" release. As I was putting the finishing touches on "Glue", I discovered that there's an artist that has evolved from this century that have really hit home with me: Coldplay. I know: most of you know me as a rocker & I listen to KSHE, The Point, & bands like Rush, Led Zeppelin, Iron Maiden, Metallica, AC/DC, & Ozzy Osbourne/Black Sabbath almost daily. But a band like Coldplay hits home for me, especially after finally seeing them in concert this past Summer in St. Louis, plus they're so inspiring to me: the melodies flow & the lyrics really hit home. Thank God for music, & the way it ignites my soul & inspires me to write every day...

9. My lucky numbers have always been 7 & 17, w/11 & 14 as "honorable mention"...

10. IF I ever won the lottery, there's 5 things I'd like to spend my money on:

   • Build a small log cabin near water &/or a mountain

- Donate to the 5 charities I mentioned above
- Donate to St. Louis University Athletic Department, & help start a Division 1 Ice Hockey program & a Division 1 Football program...& donate to SLU Medical &/or Washington University Medical, to help fund research to find a Cure for Cancer, & other debilitating medical issues, & mental illnesses as well
- Become a shareholder of the St. Louis Blues, &/or bring a Major League Soccer franchise to St. Louis
- Help out as many people that have touched my life that I can

## My last thought(s) for "Glue"...

I'm a HUGE Peanut's fan & I absolutely love **Snoopy**--without a doubt, I'm all about "Joe Cool" & everything that wonderful fictional Beagle stands for. However, I feel my life is very parallel to his best friend, **Charlie Brown**, more so than any other fictional character ever created. Charles Schulz is spot on in most of the messages & analogies he conveyed to his followers throughout his career & in the present day.

As a life-long fan, I finally watched "The Peanuts Movie" not long ago, with my heart & mind totally focused on the storyline, more so than the great "modernization" of the animation. Some people have compared me to Charlie Brown in the past, &-- for the first time EVER--I truly felt I'm his carbon copy. Our personality traits mirror one another's...plus, we have our faithful dog by our side always. Yes, I've been a "blockhead" at times, I tend to "over-think" some situations, & I've always second guessed myself about being "good enough". But-- deep down--I'm just like "good ol' Chuck": a guy with a heart of gold, who puts others in front of himself for their benefit, who never gives up & always tries to find the good in every situation. Yup--that's me...the "modern day Charlie Brown": a good guy that's always "glued" together.

Thank YOU, my friend, for reading "Glue"... I hope you enjoyed the ride.